Forest Green *Glass*

Philip Hopper

Schiffer Publishing Ltd®

4880 Lower Valley Road, Atglen, PA 19310 USA

Dedication

The inspiration for this book came from Barbara W. Birge of Lexington, Kentucky. No other person has had such a profound effect on my life. I have learned the meaning of true love and commitment, found another person to share and expand my passion (maybe I should have said obsession) with "collecting", and realized there is another person who lives "in" the world, not "on" the world. Barbara is in tune with everything that goes on around her. She doesn't allow the daily chores to cloud her enjoyment of the simple things in life. . . . the sound of the crickets at night, hearing the water as it cascades over the rocks in a brook, the mellow hoot of an owl looking for a mate, the wind rustling through the trees, the sight of a thunderstorm and lightning in the distant sky, or the contentment of sitting with someone special while watching the dramatic color changes occurring as the sun sets in the evening. These are the special things that we have learned to appreciate and share. I thank God every day for finding such a special person and I sincerely hope others will have the same experiences.

Copyright © 2000 by Philip Hopper
Library of Congress Catalog Card Number: 99-67494

Designed by Bonnie M. Hensley
Type set in Korrina

ISBN: 0-7643-1058-5
Printed in China
1 2 3 4

Published by Schiffer Publishing Ltd.
4880 Lower Valley Road
Atglen, PA 19310
Phone: (610) 593-1777; Fax: (610) 593-2002
E-mail: Schifferbk@aol.com
Please visit our web site catalog at **www.schifferbooks.com**

In Europe, Schiffer books are distributed by Bushwood Books
6 Marksbury Avenue
Kew Gardens
Surrey TW9 4JF England
Phone: 44 (0)208-392-8585; Fax: 44 (0)208-392-9876
E-mail: Bushwd@aol.com

This book may be purchased from the publisher.
Include $3.95 for shipping. Please try your bookstore first.
We are interested in hearing from authors with book ideas on related subjects.
You may write for a free printed catalog.

$\mathscr{C}$ontents

Acknowledgments 4
Notes for Collectors 5
A History of Anchor Hocking 7
Introduction 9
Chapter One   Patterns 11
Chapter Two   Vases 45
Chapter Three   Pitchers and Glasses 55
Chapter Four   Relish Trays/Lazy Susans 85
Chapter Five   Lamps 90
Chapter Six   Bowls 91
Chapter Seven   Ash Trays 98
Chapter Eight   Miscellaneous/Novelty Items 101
Chapter Nine   Confusing Similarities 108
Chapter Ten   Advertising Sheets 111
                        Index   112

Acknowledgments

You never know where life is going. I never dreamed that I would ever be known for my writing talents, but this is what has happened. Who do I have to thank for that??? The answer lies at Bennett Junior High School in Manchester, Connecticut. When I took English in eighth grade, I was stunned when I earned a "D" the first quarter. At the time I thought the teacher (Mrs. Miller) was tough, mean, and downright sadistic. Little did I know that she would have a tremendous influence on my life. When I finally got the courage to face my parents with the first and only "D" I ever earned, my mother called Mrs. Miller. Now I must explain that Mrs. Miller didn't "give" me the "D", I "earned" it. There is a distinct difference. Anyway, my mother immediately called Mrs. Miller and they decided I would stay after school two days a week for "extra help." I envisioned it as torture, but they had more insight than a white haired, pudgy eighth grader. For three months I stayed after school. I spent the first 30 minutes writing about anything. I could choose to describe my cat, tell a funny story, write about what I did on vacation, or any other subject that came to mind. Then Mrs. Miller would sit beside me and I would first read what I wrote aloud. You really never realize how bad you writing is until you read it aloud!! Then she would ask me what I could do to make the sentence structure better, make it flow more smoothly, and really express what I wanted to say. Three months of pure Hell and I was finally let off the hook.

To this day, there is just no way to adequately express my appreciation to Mrs. Miller and my mother for their insight and dedication to my welfare. Mrs. Miller was a dedicated teacher, a rarity in this day and age, and my mother was a loving, caring parent. Working together they made sure I had all the skills necessary to thrive in life. I thank them both for their dedication!!

Special thanks goes out to Sondra Reger of Finksburg, Maryland, for finding numerous pieces of glassware for me. She located auctions on eBay that I missed, searched out antique shops I could never visit, and kept an eye out for something "special" for the books. My sincere appreciation for all her efforts!

Every Saturday and Sunday morning I drive my 1964 Ford Thunderbird on its weekly "outing" to a local restaurant. This is a ritual I have made for almost three years. One morning my usual server, Mary E. Burt, presented me with a paper bag filled with Forest Green Sandwich glass. Mary is not a collector. She is just an incredibly kind, thoughtful person who cared enough to buy the glass for me. She wasn't sure if I needed the pieces, wasn't sure if they were made by Anchor Hocking, and wasn't sure if they were actually Forest Green. She did know that I talked about writing a book about Anchor Hocking Forest Green glassware and that was good enough for her. She took the time out of her busy schedule to locate and purchase the glass. This is the real reward for writing books . . . . meeting "special" people like Mary!

I was very lucky to finally find someone who could point me in the right direction about the Forest Green Tumblers with the pictures and signatures. Mickey Fisher, coordinator of the Ruth Lyons Children's Fund and employee of WLWT-TV in Cincinnati, Ohio, provided the information about The 50-50 Club, which aired on WLW radio. With her help, I hope I can identify all the personalities pictured on the glasses and further document the life of Ruth Lyons, a "living legend" of radio.

Finally, I want to thank Chuck Smith, Primary Superintendent for Anchor Hocking Consumer Glass Company, for taking the time out of his hectic schedule to provide me with the glass formulations for Forest Green, Avocado Green, and Spearmint Green glass. The information is an interesting part of glassmaking so often overlooked in most reference books.

Notes for Collectors

For those who are just starting in this field, a few notes and suggestions learned from years of collecting may be helpful.

Pricing

The prices in the book are only a guide. They are retail prices for mint condition glassware. Several factors will have an effect of glassware prices: regional availability, depth and consistency in coloring, the presence or absence of Anchor Hocking markings in the glass or as paper labels, and relative rarity of the piece. Certain items will command higher prices if they are sets in the original packaging. I would also consider labeled pieces (paper or marks embedded in the glass) to command a 10 to 20 percent increase in price over unmarked pieces. Prices will drop considerably for glassware that is chipped, scratched, cracked, or deformed. No matter what any reference book states, the bottom line is . . .

Glassware is only worth what someone is willing to pay for it!

Measurements

I have tried to make this reference book as "user friendly" as possible. Too many times I have been in an antique shop and spotted a tumbler I wanted. The reference book I was using said this was a 12 oz. tumbler. Without a container of liquid and measuring cup I would have no way to actually determine if the tumbler held 12 ounces. I would rather know the tumbler is 5 inches high with a top diameter of 3 inches. This I can measure with a ruler. Unless otherwise noted, the measurements listed in the book are the height of the item. Realize, throughout the production of certain glassware items, the mold dimensions did vary. The measurements in the book are the actual measurements made on the each piece of glassware pictured.

Regional Availability

Over the last seven years I have noticed regional differences in the availability of the majority of Anchor Hocking glassware. Many items produced by Anchor Hocking were used as promotional items and therefore, were regionally distributed. These items were not listed in the catalog or "jobber" sheets used by sales personnel. For example, Whirly Twirly bowls in both Forest Green and Royal Ruby are quite common in the east, but virtually rare on the midwest. This local availability will definitely affect pricing!

Resources Available to Collectors

Collectors today have a great variety of resources available. With the advent of the "electronic age," collecting capabilities have been greatly expanded. I can honestly state this book would not have been possible without using the vast resources available, especially on the internet. Below I have listed the resources collectors can use for locating antiques and glassware, however, realize this list is not all inclusive.

Internet Resources: Without leaving the comfort of your home or office, you can search worldwide for items to add to your collection. Presently, there are both antique dealers and auctions services on the internet.

eBay Auction Service: The eBay Auction Service provides a continually changing source of items. This internet service contains over 2,000,000 items in 371 categories. Internet users can register as both buyers and/or sellers. The majority of the items remain on the "auction block" for seven days. You can search the auction database for specific items. A list of items will be presented following the search. For example, you might want to find a Fire King Jadite vase made by Anchor Hocking. Because the seller enters the item's description in the database, you often have to anticipate how the item is described. Don't limit the searches. In this case, you might have to search under jadite, hocking, fireking (no space), fire king (with the space), or vase to find the item you want.

Internet Antique Malls: There are several internet antique malls I have found to be extremely useful in locating glassware. Each mall contains numerous individual dealers with items for sale. The malls I used are listed below:

1. TIAS Mall – (http://www.tias.com/)
2. Collector Online Mall – (http: // www . collectoronline . com/)
3. Facets Mall – (http: // www . facets.net / facets /

shopindx .htm)
4. Depression Era Glass and China Megashow – (http:
   // www . glassshow . com /)
5. Cyberattic Antiques and Collectibles – (http: //
   cyberattic . com/)

Glass shows, antique shops and flea markets: All collectors still enjoy searching the deep dark crevices of the local antique shops and flea markets. Many of the best "finds" in my personal collection were located in flea markets and "junk" shops. Most of the dealers in glass shows have a good working knowledge of glassware, so "real finds" are not too plentiful.

Periodicals: Both the *Depression Glass Magazine* and *The Daze, Inc.* are periodicals which will greatly enhance your collecting abilities. Along with the numerous advertisements for glassware, there are informative articles on all facets of collecting glassware.

Websites: I have set up a website, http: // home . swbell . net / rrglass, to convey information about Anchor Hocking glassware. As time goes on, the information will be expanded to include photographs of rare items, unidentified items, and general company information.

Word of Mouth: This is one resource so often overlooked. Let others know what you are looking for. Consider expanding you search by including friends, relatives, and other collectors. This book could not have been written without the help of many fellow collectors.

Do not limit you collecting to only one resource. Remember the items you seek are out there...somewhere!

Request for Additional Information

I am always seeking information concerning Anchor Hocking's glassware production. Much of the information about the company is not available in a printed format. This book will undoubtedly be updated and it is imperative new information be made available to collectors. If you have any information you would like to share with the "collector world," please contact me at the following address:

Philip L. Hopper
6126 Bear Branch
San Antonio, Texas 78222
E-mail: rrglass@swbell.net

Please be patient if you need a response. I am not in the glassware business. I am a military officer first and a collector the rest of the time. I will make every effort to provide prompt feedback on you inquiries. Include a self-addressed, stamped envelope if you desire a written response.

A History of Anchor Hocking

Anchor Hocking first came into existence when Isaac J. Collins and six friends raised $8,000 to buy the Lancaster Carbon Company when it went into receivership in 1905. The company's facility was known as the "Black Cat" from all the carbon dust. Mr. Collins, a native of Salisbury, Maryland, had been working in the decorating department of the Ohio Flint Glass Company when this opportunity arose. Unfortunately the $8,000 that was raised was not sufficient to purchase and operate the new company, so Mr. Collins enlisted the help of Mr. E. B. Good. With a check for $17,000 provided by Mr. Good, one building, two day-tanks, and 50 employees, Mr. Collins was able to begin operations at the Hocking Glass Company.

The company, named for the Hocking River near which the plant was located, made and sold approximately $20,000 worth of glassware in the first year. Production was expanded with the purchase of another day-tank. This project was funded by selling $5,000 in stock to Thomas Fulton, who was to become the Secretary-Treasurer of Hocking Glass Company.

Just when everything seemed to be going well, tragedy struck the company. In 1924 the Black Cat was reduced to ashes by a tremendous fire. Mr. Collins and his associates were not discouraged. They managed to raise the funding to build what is known as Plant 1 on top of the ashes of the Black Cat. This facility was specifically designed for the production of glassware. Later in that same year, the company also purchased controlling interest in the Lancaster Glass Company (later called Plant 2) and the Standard Glass Manufacturing Company with plants in Bremen and Canal Winchester, Ohio.

The development of a revolutionary machine that pressed glass automatically saved the company when the Great Depression hit. The new machine raised production rates from 1 item per minute to over 30 items per minute. When the 1929 stock market crash hit, the company responded by developing a 15-mold machine, which could produce 90 pieces of blown glass per minute. This allowed the company to sell tumblers "two for a nickel" and survive the depression when so many other companies vanished.

Hocking Glass Company entered the glass container business in 1931 with the purchase of 50% of the General Glass Company, which in turn acquired Turner Glass Company of Winchester, Indiana. In 1934, the company developed the first one-way beer bottle.

Anchor Hocking Glass Corporation came into existence on December 31, 1937 when the Anchor Cap and Closure Corporation and its subsidiaries merged with the Hocking Glass Company. The Anchor Cap and Closure Corporation had closure plants in Long Island City, New York and Toronto, Canada, and glass container plants in Salem, New Jersey and Connelsville, Pennsylvania.

Anchor Hocking Glass Corporation continued to expand into other areas of production such as tableware, closure and sealing machinery, and toiletries and cosmetic containers through the expansion of existing facilities and the purchase of Baltimore, Maryland-based Carr-Lowry Glass Company and Maywood Glass on the west coast. In the 1950s, the corporation established the Research and Development Center in Lancaster, purchased the Tropical Glass and Container Company in Jacksonville, Florida, and built a new facility in San Leandro, California in 1959.

In 1962, the company build a new glass container plant in Houston, Texas while also adding a second unit to the Research and Development Center, known as the General Development Laboratory. In 1963 Zanesville Mold Company in Ohio became an Anchor Hocking Corporation subsidiary. The company designed and manufactured mold equipment for Anchor Hocking.

The word "Glass" was dropped from the company's name in 1969 because the company had evolved into an international company with an infinite product list. They had entered the plastic market in 1968 with the acquisition of Plastics Incorporated in St. Paul, Minnesota. They continued to expand their presence in the plastic container market with the construction of a plant in Springdale, Ohio. This plant was designed to produce blown mold plastic containers. Anchor Hocking Corporation entered the lighting field in September 1970 with the purchase of Phoenix Glass Company in Monaca, Pennsylvania. They also bought the Taylor, Smith & Taylor Company, located in Chester, West Virginia, to make earthenware, fine stoneware, institutional china dinnerware, and commemorative collector plates.

Over the years, several changes occurred in the company. Phoenix Glass Company was destroyed by fire on 15 July 1978, Shenango China (new Castle, Pennsylvania) was purchased in 28 March 1979, Taylor, Smith & Taylor was sold on 30 September 1981, and on 1 April 1983 the company decided to divest its interest in the Glass Container Division to an affiliate of the Wesray Corporation. The Glass Container Division was to be known as the Anchor Glass Container Corporation with seven manufacturing plants and its office in Lancaster, Ohio.

Anchor Hocking Corporation was acquired by the Newell Corporation on 2 July 1987. With this renewed influx of capital, several facilities were upgraded and some less profitable facilities were either closed or sold. The Clarksburg, West Virginia facility was closed in November 1987, Shenango China was sold on 22 January 1988, and Carr-Lowry Glass was sold on 12 October 1989. Today, Anchor Hocking enjoys the financial backing and resources as one of the 18 decentralized Newell Companies that manufacture and market products in four basic markets: housewares, hardware, home furnishings, and office products. You may recognize such familiar Newell Companies such as Intercraft, Levolor Home Fashions, Anchor Hocking Glass, Goody Products, Anchor Hocking Specialty Glass, Sanford, Stuart Hall, Newell Home Furnishings, Amerock, BerzOmatic, or Lee/Rowan.

ntroduction

Producing the Green Color

Over the years Anchor Hocking has made several colors of green glassware. The most notable colors are Forest Green, Avocado Green, and Spearmint Green. The basic green color in the glass is due to the presence of chromium metal. Variations in the hues of the green colors is determined by the other oxidized metals present.

Forest Green was produced in the late 1950s and continued into the mid 1960s. The glass "batch" was produced by adding 52 pounds of iron chromite mix to each ton of sand. The iron chromite mix consisted of 200 pounds of iron chromite (iron chromium oxide, $FeCr_2O_4$), 152 pounds of soda ash (sodium carbonate, Na_2CO_3), and 48 pounds of red copper oxide (Cu_2O). The final glass contained 0.272 percent iron III oxide (Fe_2O_3), 0.41 percent chromium III oxide (Cr_2O_3), and 0.24 percent copper I oxide (Cu_2O).

Avocado Green was introduced in the late 1960s and produced into the early 1970s. It was a yellow green, highly oxidized glass produced using only 7 ounces of a 3.0 percent cobalt oxide mix, 2 pounds 12 ounces of potassium bichromate ($Cr_2K_2O_7$), and 9 ounces of nickel oxide (NiO) per ton of sand. The final glass contained 0.050 percent chromium III oxide (Cr_2O_3), 0.0006 percent cobalt oxide (Co_3O_4), and 0.018 percent nickel oxide (Ni_2O_3).

Finally, Spearmint Green was produced in the late 1970s. This color was an intermediate color between Forest Green and Avocado Green made using 14 pounds of the iron chromite mix (also used in Forest Green) and 10 ounces of black copper II oxide (CuO) per ton of sand. The resulting glass contained 0.110 percent chromium III oxide (Cr_2O_3) and 0.022 percent copper I oxide (Cu_2O).

The colors can be reasonably distinguished when placed in close proximity to each other; however, light spectral curves is the only method that will definitively distinguish between Forest Green, Avocado Green, and Spearmint Green glassware.

Catalog Identification

Anchor Hocking used a series of numbers and letters to denote glassware identification in the catalogs. Starting with a basic design number, the company placed a letter (prefix) in front of the number to denote the color and cut or glass type selection. There are some excep-

tions to this identification scheme and the capacities listed in the catalog are not based on the item being filled to the rim. The following is a listing of the letter designations generally used throughout the catalogs:

No prefix:	Crystal
E:	Forest Green
F:	Laser Blue
H:	Crystal Fire King
J:	Cut Glass
L:	Luster Shell
N:	Honey Gold
R:	Royal Ruby
T:	Avocado
Y:	Spicy Brown
W:	White

For pitchers and glasses, each item of a particular pattern was given its own designation to indicate the capacity. Below are the common capacity designations:

63:	6 oz. fruit juice
65:	11 oz. tumbler
69:	15 oz. iced tea
92:	19 oz. large iced tea
93:	22 oz. giant iced tea
3375:	32 oz. giant sized ice tea
86:	86 oz. capacity of pitcher

The patterns were also given specific designations. Below is a listing of some common Forest Green pattern designations:

325:	Colonial Lady
351:	Leaf Design
352:	Polka Dots
5612:	Spinning Wheel and Churn
5613:	Wild Geese
5614:	Floral and Diamond
5615:	Gazelle
5705:	Gold and White Vintage
5807:	White Lace

Putting this all together, the #E92/5612 would indicate a Forest Green tumbler (E), 19 oz. large iced tea (92), in the Spinning Wheel and Churn pattern (5612).

Identification Marks

Over the years Anchor Hocking has used several identification marks to mark their glassware. In 1980, the company issued a limited edition 75th anniversary ashtray, pictured below, which portrays the corporate identification marks. During the photographing, the marks on the ashtray were blackened with a magic marker so they would show up when photographed.

Originally, when the Hocking Glass Company was established in 1905, the company used the mark seen on the left side of the ashtray. This mark was used from 1905 until 1937, when it was replaced by the more familiar anchor over H mark (center of ashtray) to illustrate the merger of the Hocking Glass Company and the Anchor Cap Company. Finally, in October 1977, the company adopted a new symbol (right side of the ashtray), an anchor with a modern, contemporary appearance to further the new corporate identity.

75th Anniversary ashtray.

Crystal ashtray, 5-1/2" in diameter, $50-55 with original box.

Paper label for the Gay Fad Studios located in Lancaster, Ohio. The label states "Gay Fad hand decorated, fired for permanency." This is the only Gay Fad label I have seen and it was attached to a Hazel Atlas pitcher.

Chapter 1

Patterns

Baltic

The commonly found items are the "footed" glasses and sherbets. The 12 oz. footed bowls, while not as common, were listed in the 1971Anchor Hocking catalog, but shown in crystal only.

Baltic tumblers. Left: 10 oz. goblet #E3316, 4-1/2", $8-10; right: 5 oz. juice #E3311, 3-5/8", $5-8.

Listing for the Baltic Pattern in the 1971 Anchor Hocking catalog.

The Baltic 6-1/2 oz. sherbet #E3313, 2-3/8", $5-8; 6-1/4" plate #E828, $8-10.

Baltic 6-1/2 oz. sherbet #E3313 with an etched tulip, 2-3/8", $10-12.

Belmont

This pattern was listed in the institutional glassware catalogs in the late 1960s and only in crystal. While there are several sizes in crystal, I have only been able to find one size in Forest Green.

10-1/2 oz. Belmont tumbler #E3145, 5", $12-15.

1967 Anchor Hocking Institutional Glassware Catalog listing the Belmont tumblers.

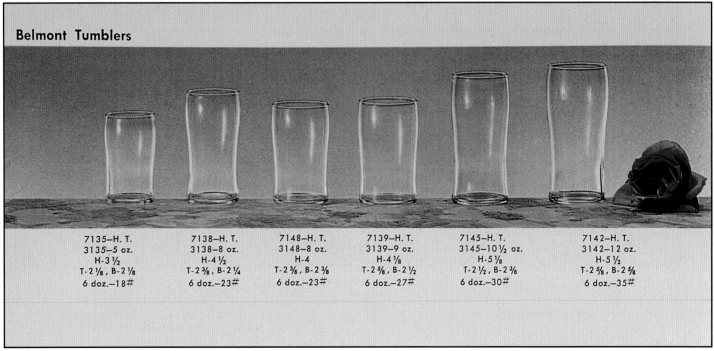

Belmont Tumblers

7135–H. T.	7138–H. T.	7148–H. T.	7139–H. T.	7145–H. T.	7142–H. T.
3135–5 oz.	3138–8 oz.	3148–8 oz.	3139–9 oz.	3145–10½ oz.	3142–12 oz.
H-3 ½	H-4 ½	H-4	H-4 ⅛	H-5 ⅛	H-5 ½
T-2 ⅛, B-2 ⅛	T-2 ⅜, B-2 ¼	T-2 ⅜, B-2 ⅜	T-2 ⅝, B-2 ½	T-2 ½, B-2 ⅜	T-2 ⅝, B-2 ⅝
6 doz.–18#	6 doz.–23#	6 doz.–23#	6 doz.–27#	6 doz.–30#	6 doz.–35#

Beverly

This pattern was made in six sizes of glasses. The catalog lists the glasses in crystal and I have only been able to find nine of the 4-1/2 oz cocktails in Royal Ruby and five of the 9 oz. old fashioneds in Forest Green.

Anchor Hocking listed six pieces of Beverly in the 1971 catalog. I have only been able to find the 4-1/2 oz. cocktail in Royal Ruby and the 9 oz. old fashioned in Forest Green.

Beverly 9 oz. old fashioned #E3265, 3-1/2", $20-25. Notice there is a handle that can be snapped on the glass to make the glass serve as a cup.

Burple

Anchor Hocking only made the 4-1/2" and 8" bowls in the Burple pattern. They were sold as the Burple Dessert Set which included one 8" and six 4-1/2" bowls. The bowls are common in crystal and green, but relatively rare in Royal Ruby. Some of the crystal bowls were entirely acid etched to create a "frosted" appearance.

Burple glassware has a very distinctive pattern. Here is the 8" berry bowl
#E1878, $25-35, and the 4-1/2" dessert bowl #E1874, $10-12.

Anchor Hocking sold this pattern as the Burple Dessert
Set consisting of one 8" and six 4-1/2" bowls, $70-75.

Charm

Charm (square) dinnerware was produced in the 1950s and given the E-2200 designation by Anchor Hocking. There are several references to the 9-1/4" dinner plate in Royal Ruby, but I have been unable to confirm its existence. With the exception of the platter, most of the pieces are relatively common in Forest Green.

Cup #E2279, $2-5; saucer #E2229, 5-3/8", $5-10.

Left to right: dinner plate #E2244, 9-1/4", $25-35; luncheon plate #E2241, 8-3/8", $12-15; salad plate #E2237, 6-5/8", $10-16.

Charm was listed in the 1952 catalog.

FOREST GREEN PARTY SERVICE
MODERN DESIGN AND COLOR

E2279
CUP
Packs 6 doz.—26#

E2229
SAUCER
Packs 6 doz.—30#

E2275 — 4¾"
DESSERT OR CEREAL
Packs 6 doz.—34#

E2241 — 8⅜"
LUNCHEON PLATE
Packs 3 doz.—42#

ATTRACTIVE YET LOW-PRICED
FOREST GREEN LUNCHEON SERVICE

E2200/11 — 16 Pce. Luncheon Set
Each Set Pkd. in Gift Ctn., 4 Sets to R/S Ctn.—43#

COMPOSITION:
Four Cups
Four Saucers
Four Desserts
Four Luncheon Plates

Gift Packed

Left: creamer #E2254, $12-15; right: sugar #E2253,
$12-15. Notice the creamer has an acid etched tulip design.

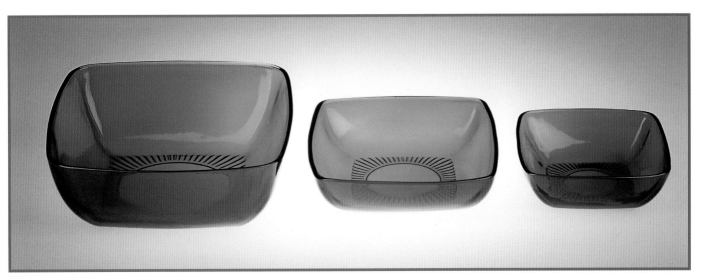

Left to right: salad bowl #E2277, 7-1/2", $20-30; soup bowl #E2267,
6", $12-15; dessert or cereal bowl #E2275, 4-5/8", $10-12.

Platter #E2247, 8" x 11",
$30-45.

Early American

Although Anchor Hocking gave this stemware the name Early American, collectors still use the name "bubble." Early American was made in a 13 oz. ice tea, 9-1/2 oz. goblet, 6 oz. sherbet, 5-1/2 oz. juice, and 4-1/2 oz. cocktail. Crystal and Forrest Green pieces were made in all five sizes. The 13 oz. ice tea was not produced in Royal Ruby, but was produced in crystal, crystal with 22 kt. gold trim, and Forest Green. The shape of the bowl, stem, and base differs from both the Berwick and Inspiration stemware. Quite common four or five years ago, Early American stemware has virtually disappeared because it makes a popular table setting during the Christmas holiday season.

Left to right: 16 oz goblet in crystal, 6", $20-30 in Forest Green; 10 oz. goblet #E336, 5-1/4", $15-20; 4-1/2 oz. fruit juice #E335, 4-1/4", $12-15; 6 oz. sherbet #E333, 4", $12-15; 3-1/2 oz. cocktail #E334, 3-3/8", $18-20.

Anchor Hocking produced two types of Forest Green and crystal stemware. There are several differences between the stem of the Early American (bubble) on the left and the Inspiration on the right. The shape of the stem and the number and type of "bumps" on the two bases vary considerably.

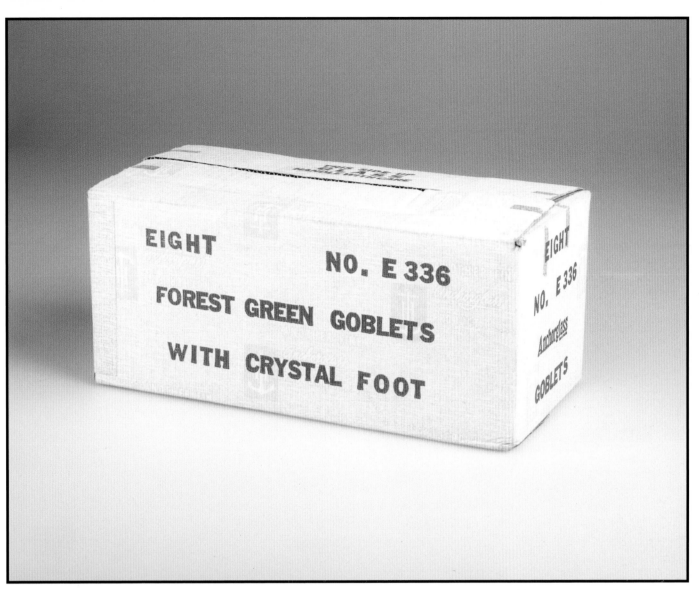

Box containing eight Early American 10 oz. goblets #E336, 5-1/4", $125-150, $20-25 for the box alone.

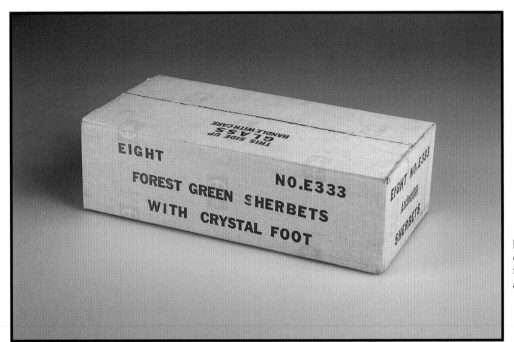

Box containing eight Early American 6 oz. sherbets #E333, 4", $125-150, $20-25 for the box alone.

19

The Georgian pattern was probably produced from the 1940s to the 1970s, but not continuously throughout this period. Unlike many of the other patterns of Forest Green, some of the tumblers have the "anchor over H" emblem embedded in the bottom of the glass. There are six sizes of tumblers in Royal Ruby, but only one size in Forest Green. The tumblers tend to chip very easily, therefore, mint pieces will command a premium price.

Georgian 9 oz. tumbler #E49, 4-1/4", $12-15.

Catalog page from the 1964 catalog showing the Georgian pattern in Forest Green.

Inspiration

The Inspiration pattern was not part of Anchor Hocking's open stock. Most of the Inspiration glassware was given away as promotional items. Forest Green is the usual color found in this pattern. In addition to the glasses, two sizes of plates were produced: an 8" salad or luncheon plate and 6-1/4" sherbet plate. Both plates have the same swirled design found on the foot of the glasses.

Left to right: 13 oz. iced tea, 6-5/8", $15-20; 11 oz. goblet, 5-7/8", $12-15; 4-1/2 oz. juice, 4-1/2", $12-15; 6 oz. sherbet, 3-3/4", $12-15.

Most the sizes of Inspiration were also sold with 22 kt. gold on the rim. These glasses would command a 10-20 percent increase in price.

13 oz. iced tea with etched "W", 6-5/8", $25-30.

Inspiration plates. Left: 8" plate, $12-15; right: 6-1/4" plate with etched leaves, $15-20.

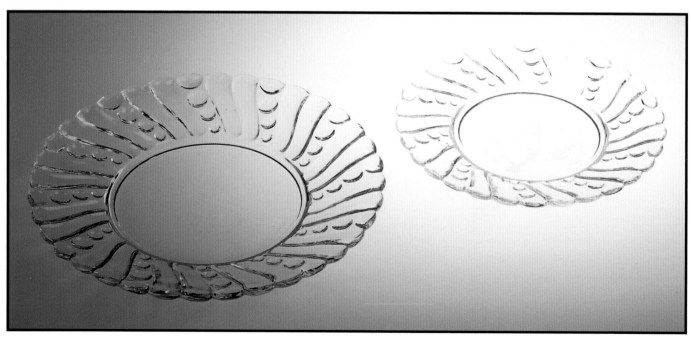

Milano

Milano was made for several years and in numerous colors such as Avocado Green, Honey Gold, Crystal, Forest Green, Laser Blue, Spicy Brown, and Aquamarine. Anchor Hocking made one size of pitcher and at least eight sizes of glasses. The pattern was called Milano in the 1960s and Lido in the 1970s.

Left: Milano 3 qt. ice lip pitcher #E4087, $30-40; right: 12 oz. tumbler #E4012, 5-1/2", $10-12.

Anchor Hocking listed the Forest Green pitcher and two sizes of glasses in the 1964 catalog; however, the 1963 catalog lists four sizes of tumblers. Later catalogs also list this pattern as Lido.

milano

crystal ice

4005	5 oz juice • 3 dz/shipper/12 lbs	.75 dz
4007	7 oz old-fash • 3 dz/shipper/15 lbs	.95 dz
4010	10 oz tumbler • 3 dz/shipper/22 lbs	.95 dz
4012	12 oz tumbler • 3 dz/shipper/23 lbs	.95 dz
4015	15 oz tumbler • 3 dz/shipper/25 lbs	1.20 dz
4087	3 qt ice lip pitcher • ½ dz/shipper/20 lbs	4.75 dz
4000/41	9 pc refreshment set • C/D ctn •	
	4 sets/shipper/32 lbs	1.40 set
	8 (4012) tumblers • (4087) pitcher	

pillar packs • 4 pc sets

4005-D	5 oz juice • 12 sets/shipper/18 lbs	.28 set
4007-D	7 oz old-fash • 12 sets/shipper/23 lbs	.36 set
4012-D	12 oz tumbler • 12 sets/shipper/35 sets	.39 set

forest green

E4012	12 oz tumbler • 3 dz/shipper/23 lbs	.95 dz
E4015	15 oz tumbler • 3 dz/shipper/25 lbs	1.20 dz
E4087	3 qt ice lip pitcher • ½ dz/shipper/20 lbs	4.75 dz

milk-white

W553	9 oz tumbler • 3 dz/shipper/21 lbs	1.20 dz
W548	72 oz pitcher • ½ dz/shipper/19 lbs	7.75 dz
W500/55	7 pc set • gift ctn • 6 sets/shipper/43 lbs	1.45 set
	6 (W553) tumblers • (W548) pitcher	

Provincial

Forest Green Provincial, commonly known as "bubble" by collectors, was designated as the E-1600 series that was produced from 1953 until the mid-1960s. Most of the Provincial pieces are marked with paper labels, however, I have found the Royal Ruby 12 oz. tumbler #R1612, 6 oz. fruit juice #R1606, and the 8" and 4-1/2" bowls with the "anchor over H" emblem embedded in the glass. Mint condition plates are difficult to find because the edges are thin and easily chipped. The Forest Green candleholders are relatively difficult to find.

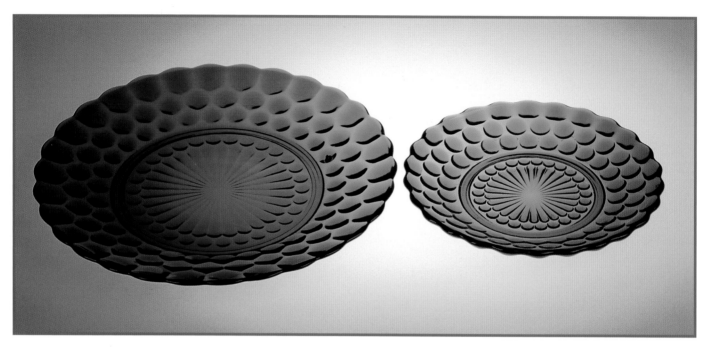

Dinner plate #E1641, 9-1/4", $30-35;
salad plate, 6-1/2", $25-35.

Left to right: vegetable bowl #E1678, 8-1/4", $75-100; cereal bowl #E1665, 5-1/4", $20-25; dessert bowl #E1664, 4-1/2", $8-12.

Cup #E1650, $5-10; saucer #E1628, 5-1/2", $5-10.

Left: creamer, $20-25; right: sugar, $20-25.

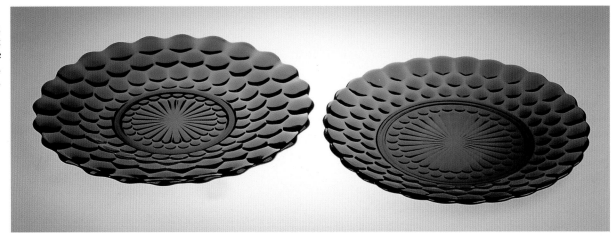

Left: large platter, 9-7/8", $30-40; right: dinner plate #E1641, 9-1/4", $30-35.

Advertisement for the Provincial pattern.

Aftermarket scale made with two #E1665 cereal bowls. The
Novelty Crystal Corporation, 79-55 Albion Avenue, Elmhurst,
New York made the remaining parts of the scale; however, they
did not assemble the scale.

Queen Mary

The Queen Mary pattern, produced from 1936-1949, is usually found in crystal and pink. The pattern is also called "vertical ribbed" by collectors. The 3-1/2" round coaster ash tray was made in Forest Green in the 1950s and is common today.

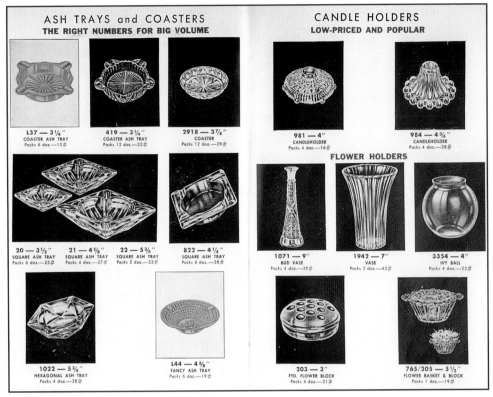

The 1952 Anchor Hocking catalog listed the Queen Mary coaster ashtray.

Aftermarket Statue of Liberty souvenir which used the Queen Mary ashtray coaster, $40-50.

Queen Mary coaster ashtray #E419, 3-1/4", $8-10.

Roly Poly

This pattern was undoubtedly made for several years. Given the E3600 designation, Roly Poly was sold in a number of different refreshment and tumbler sets. The 1971 catalog lists two other sizes of Roly Poly, the 9 oz. on-the-rocks and the 6 oz. juice. These are listed in crystal in the catalog but they may exist in Forest Green.

Left to right: 96 oz. upright pitcher #E3687, $40-50; 13 oz. beverage/ice tea #E3658, 5", $8-10; 9 oz. table tumbler #E3651, 4-1/4", $8-10; 5 oz. fruit juice #E3653, 3-3/8", $5-8.

9-Piece Refreshment Set #E3600/77, $100-125 for the complete set in the box; $20-25 for the box only. Notice this box could be used for both the Royal Ruby (#R3600/2) and Forest Green (#E3600/77) Refreshment Sets.

Overhead view of the 9-Piece Refreshment Set so you can see how the pitcher and glasses are arranged in the box.

Refreshment set removed from the box. Notice only the pitcher had a paper label.

Gay Nineties Set consists of 13 oz. beverage ice teas #E3658. Left to right: "A Bicycle for Two" tumbler, 5", $10-12; "Gas Buggy" tumbler, 5", $10-15; "Open Sleigh" tumbler 5", $10-15; "The Hansom" tumbler, 5", $10-12.

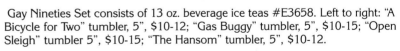

96 oz. Upright pitcher #E3687 with etched tulips, $60-75.

13 oz. Beverage/ice tea #E3658 transportation set. Left to right: "Dan and Joe" tumbler, 5", $10-12; "Early Train" tumbler, 5", $10-12; "Horse Car" tumbler, 5", $10-12.

13 oz. Beverage/ice tea glass #E3658 filled with Gill's Hotel Tea, 5", $30-35.

Closeup of the label for Gill's Hotel Tea.

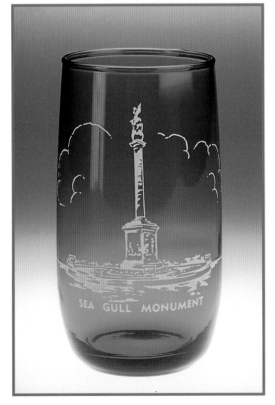

Top: 13 oz. Beverage/ice tea glasses #E3658 decorated with scenes from Tucson. Left to right: "Arizona Boys Chorus" tumbler, 5", $10-12; "Indian Bread Making Papago Tribe" tumbler, 5", $10-12, "San Xavier del Bac Mission" tumbler, 5", $10-12; "Wishing Shrine" tumbler, 5", $10-12; "Wonderland of Rocks" tumbler, 5", $10-12.

Center: 13 oz. Beverage/ice tea glasses #E3658 decorated with scenes from New Mexico. Left to right: "Ancient Mission" tumbler, 5", $10-12; "Carlsbad Caverns" tumbler, 5", $10-12; "Desert Yucca" tumbler, 5", $10-12; "Elephant Butte Lake" tumbler, 5", $10-12.

13 oz. Beverage/ice tea glass #E3658 decorated with the Sea Gull Monument, 5", $10-12.

31

Front and back of the 13 oz. beverage/ice tea glasses #E3658 decorated with applied enamel ducks and cattails, 5", $10-12.

13 oz. Beverage/ice tea glass #E3658 decorated with pictures of gazelles. Notice the lines under the gazelles are straight. There is another version with wavy lines.

9 oz. Table tumbler #E3651 from Treasure Island, Route 193, Webster, Mass., 4-1/4", $10-12.

Forest Green Sandwich glassware was produced in the 1950s. Many of the pieces of glass in this pattern are hard to find and very expensive. The two sizes of glasses were given away in boxes of oats, therefore they are quite plentiful. When the company attempted to sell pitcher and tumbler sets, the marketing strategy was not successful. Most of the sets were never sold. They were returned to the factory and probably melted down or destroyed. This would account for the relative rarity of the two pitchers and over abundance of the tumblers.

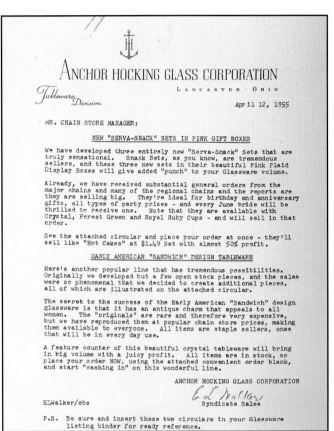

1955 Factory advertising sheet sent to store managers introducing the Sandwich pattern.

Original letter accompanying the advertising sheet.

Sandwich cup #E1479, $20-25; saucer #E1429, 5-3/4", $20-25.

Left: Sandwich sugar #E1453, $40-50; right: creamer #E1454, $40-50.

Left: Sandwich 9 oz. tumbler #E1401, 4", $8-10; right: 5 oz. fruit juice #E1403, 3", $5-8.

Sandwich dinner plate #E1441, 9", $125-150.

Sandwich cookie jar, $40-50. The Forest Green jar did not have a lid like the jars produced in the other colors of the Sandwich pattern.

Forest Green Juice Set consists of one 36 oz. juice pitcher #E1459 and six 5 oz. fruit juice glasses #E1403, $350-450 for the entire set, $50-75 for the box only.

Sandwich 36 oz. juice pitcher #E1459, $200-250. There is also a larger 75 oz. ice lip pitcher #E1487, $400-450 (not shown).

Side view of the Forest Green Juice Set box.

Overhead view of the juice set to show that the glasses were packed on top of the pitcher.

Forest Green Juice Set removed from the box.

Left to right:
Sandwich bowls:
8" bowl #E1478,
$100-125; 7"
bowl #E1427,
$50-75; 6-1/2"
bowl #E1426,
$50-75.

Dessert bowl, 4-3/8", $10-15.

Sandwich 5 oz. sherbet, 3-5/8", $5-8;
sherbet underliner plate, 4-1/2", $5-8.

Swedish Modern

There are few references to this pattern in the catalogs. The ashtrays are listed in lustre colored blue, amber, smoke, and cranberrry. The 8" salad plate and 6-1/4" sherbet plate are listed in crystal. I was unable to find any reference to Forest Green Swedish Modern but I did locate two labeled dishes.

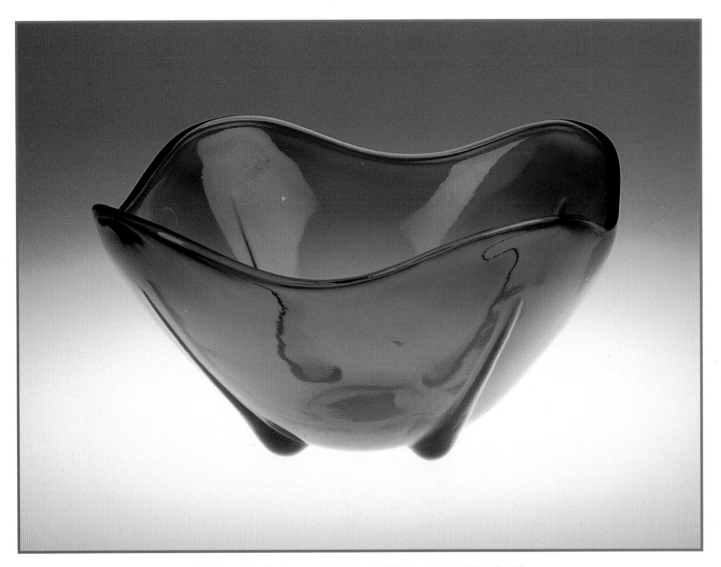

Tall Swedish Modern candy dish, 3-1/2" in height, 6-1/2" x 6-1/2",
$30-40. The dish is labeled on the *outside* bottom surface.

Short Swedish Modern candy dish, 2-1/4" in height, 6-5/8" x
6-5/8", $30-40. The dish is labeled on the *inside* bottom surface.

Swedish Modern ashtray #E6460, 5" x 5-7/8", $20-30.

Closeup of the Swedish
Modern label.

Waterford

There was a very limited production of this pattern in Forest Green. I have only found the 14" serving plate in this color. The plate was used as part of the 7-Piece Relish Service #E2900/100 which used five ivory inserts and a Forest Green sauce cup.

7-Piece Relish Service consisting of one crystal 14" serving plate, five Forest Green relish dishes (inserts), and one crystal sauce cup, $75-100 for the complete set.

7-Piece Relish Service #E2900/100 consisting of one Forest Green 14" serving plate, five Milk White relish dishes (inserts), and one Forest Green sauce cup, $75-100.

Center dish for the relish set, $12-15.

Forest Green 14" serving plate, $30-40.

Box containing the 7-Piece Relish Service #E2900/100, $25-35 for the box only.

Side view of the 7-Piece Relish Service #E2900/100 box listing the contents of the set.

E 2900/100   CONTAINS
1 - SERVING PLATE
1 - SAUCE CUP
5 - RELISH DISHES

ANCHOR HOCKING GLASS CORPORATION
LANCASTER, OHIO, U.S.A.

Whirly Twirly

Whirly Twirly glassware was produced in Forest Green, Royal Ruby, and crystal. The Forest Green glassware is relatively easy to find, while the Royal Ruby is reasonably uncommon. The pitchers are found in all three colors and the glasses in Forest Green and Royal Ruby only. Whirly Twirly (notice it is not spelled Whirley Twirley) glasses are often confused with the 9-1/2 oz. tall tumbler #R3597 and smaller juice glass. I have included side-by-side photographs to show the differences.

Left to right: 3 qt. pitcher #E3587, $50-60; 18 oz. tumbler, 6-1/2", $20-25; 12 oz. tumbler, 5", $15-20; 9 oz. tumbler, 4-1/8", $15-20; 5 oz. tumbler, 3-5/8", $10-12.

Two tumblers often confused. On the left is the Whirly Twirly 12 oz. tumbler (5" tall) and on the right is the 9-1/2 oz. tall tumbler #E3597 (4-3/4" tall). Notice the Whirly Twirly tumbler's sides are tapered and the base is footed. The E3597 tumbler has straight sides and no foot on the base.

Whirly Twirly dessert bowl, 3-3/4", $12-15.

You will notice the center dish for the relish set on the left is different in shape than the Whirly Twirly bowl on the right.

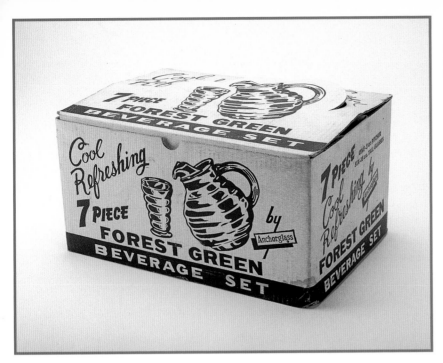

Rare Whirly Twirly Beverage Set which consists of one 3 qt. pitcher #E3587 and six 12 oz. tumblers, $500-600 for the complete set; $50-75 for the box only.

Overhead view so you can see how the pitcher and glasses are arranged in the box.

Beverage Set removed from the box.

Windsor

Anchor Hocking produced Windsor glassware in the 1940s. The 60 oz. pitcher #A1153, 9 oz. tumbler #A1131, and 5 oz. fruit juice #A1133 are generally found in Royal Ruby, the 9 oz. tumbler and 5 oz. fruit juice in crystal, and the 9 oz. tumbler in Forest Green. Some of the crystal glasses have the "anchor over H" embedded in the bottom of the glass. There may be variations in the number of rows of "cubes" on the glasses, since I have found at least three different variations in crystal and light green. Also, I have purchased a light green 4-3/4" 12 oz. tumbler with four rows of "cubes." This is a previously unknown size which may have been produced in Royal Ruby or Forest Green.

Windsor 9 oz. tumbler #E1131, 4", $10-12.

Chapter 2
Vases

Over the years, Anchor Hocking produced a variety of vases. Most of the vases were trademarked with paper labels. Some of the Royal Ruby vases have the familiar "anchor over H" emblem embedded in the glass. These are the crimped top vase #R3306, crimped bud vase #R3303, and the Rainflower vase. The trademark on the Rainflower vase is extremely hard to see, but it can be found with a magnifying glass.

Many of the vases were sold to other companies where they were etched with flowers or figures. The etching process required the piece to be first coated with paraffin wax. The de-

sign was then scraped into the wax and the piece subjected to a hydrofluoric acid mist or vapor. The acid dissolved the glass in areas not protected by the wax. After the piece was washed to remove the acid, the paraffin wax was melted off. This left the design, in white, on the surface of the glass.

The 4" ivy ball #E3354 and bud vase #E3302 were used to market either scented or mosquito repellent candles. Although only two candles are pictured, there are undoubtedly numerous other companies that made the candles. The 4" ivy ball #E3354 can be found in a variety of wall hangers.

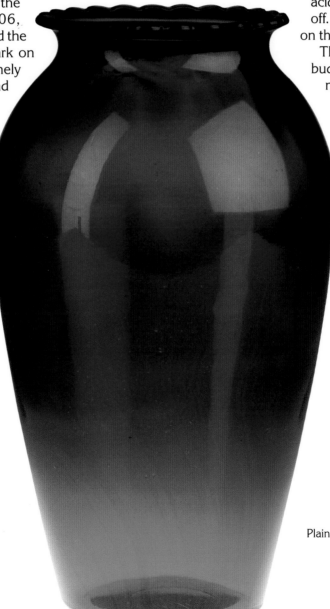

Plain vase #E53, 9", $25-40.

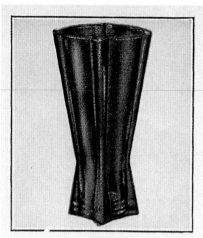

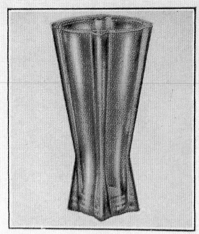

E572   M572

Catalog entry listing the two colors of the paneled "Rocket" vase. Each color is given a different name even though they appear in the same catalog.

Paneled vase #E572, 9", $30-40.

Bud vase #E3300/87, 3-3/4", $8-10. The price will vary considerably depending upon the condition of the gold decoration.

Vase #E597, 9", $25-40.

Bud vase #E3300/88, 3-3/4", $8-10. The price will vary considerably depending upon the condition of the gold decoration.

Closeup of the unusual sticker applied to the #E3302 vase.

Bud vase #E3302, 4-3/4", $8-10. Notice the unique sticker on the vase. I do not know whether Anchor Hocking or another company applied this sticker.

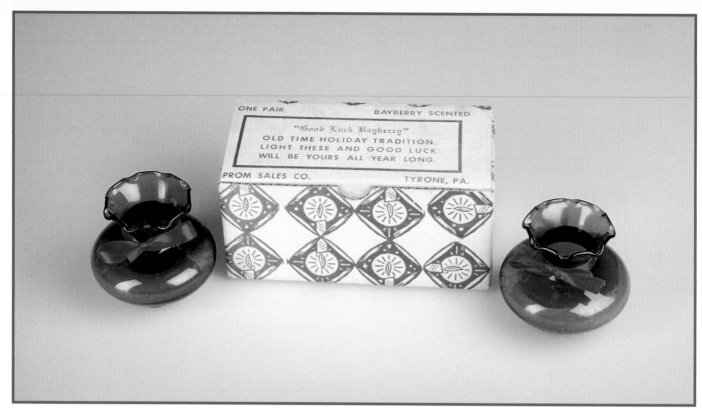

Bud vases #E3302 were sold as bayberry scented candles by the Prom Sales Company of Tyrone, Pennsylvania, $30-40 for the pair in the box.

Bud vase #E3302 with applied 22 kt. gold webbing, 4-3/4", $12-15.

Bud vase #E3302 with applied seashells that was sold as a souvenir from Florida, 4-3/4", $12-15.

Crimped top vase #E3308, 7", $12-15. This vase is easily found in Forest Green, but rarely found in Royal Ruby.

Crimped top vase #E3306, 6-1/2", $12-15.

Gift Ware set with two crimped top vases #E3306, 6-1/2", $60-75

Gift Ware set opened to show the two vases.

Crimped top vase #E3309, 8", $15-20.

Bud vase #E3310, 9", $15-20.

Plain vase #E3345, 6-3/8", $12-15 each.

Vase #E3345 with 22 kt. gold lines and applied enamel flowers, 6-3/8", $20-25 each.

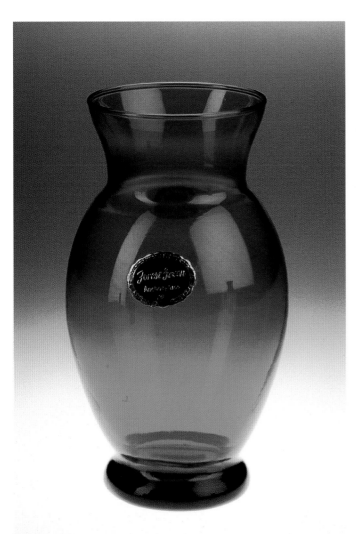

Vase #E3345 with fired on pink, 6-3/8", $25-20.

Plain vase #E3346, 6-3/8", $12-15.

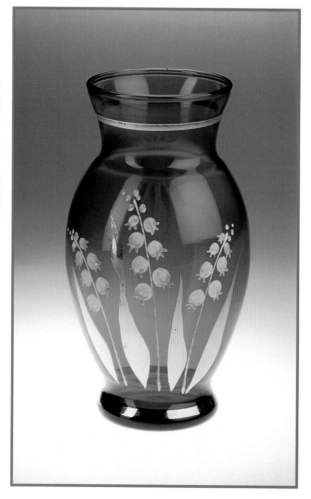

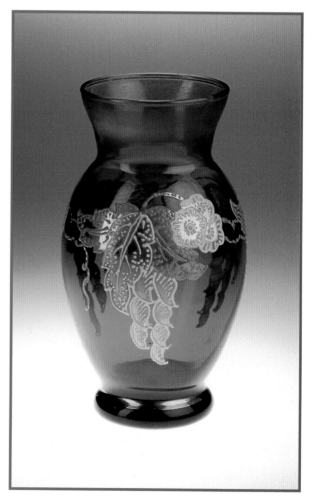

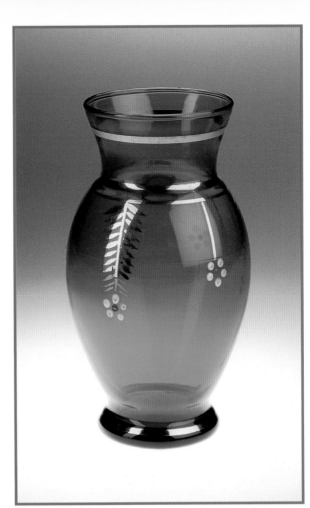

Top left: Vase #E3346 with intricate diamond cut designs, 6-3/8", $50-60.

Top right: Vase #E3346 applied enamel flowers and 22 kt. gold leaves and lines, 6-3/8", $30-40.

Left to right: small vase made by Anchor Hocking, 7", $20-25; vase made by MAPCO of Cleveland, Ohio, 10", $15-20, vase also made by MAPCO of Cleveland, Ohio, 12", $20-30.

Box containing two 4" ivy ball #E3354 Moskeeto Lites, $35-50. The Moskeeto Lites were made by the Victrylite Candle Company of Oshkosh, Wisconsin.

vases

ivy balls, flower bowls, blocks

crystal clear

3354	4" ivy ball • 4 dz/shipper/22 lbs	.75 dz
3355	4¾" ftd ivy ball • 3 dz/shipper/26 lbs	1.20 dz
3351	4½" floater • 3 dz/shipper/20 lbs	1.20 dz
1071	9" bud • 4 dz/shipper/39 lbs	.90 dz
3309	8" x 4" crimped • 2 dz/shipper/20 lbs	1.50 dz
1942	7" • 2 dz/shipper/44 lbs	2.35 dz
741	8½" Prescut • ½ dz/shipper/15 lbs	4.65 dz
742	10" Prescut • ½ dz/shipper/29 lbs	5.50 dz
203	3" 11-hole flower block • 4 dz/shipper/25 lbs	1.20 dz
205	5⅛" 16-hole flower block • 2 dz/shipper/20 lbs	1.50 dz

milk-white

W1071	9" bud • 4 dz/shipper/39 lbs	.95 dz
W58	7¼" • 2 dz/shipper/27 lbs	2.10 dz
W642	7" Vintage • 1 dz/shipper/16 lbs	3.50 dz
W542	9½" • ½ dz/shipper/11 lbs	4.15 dz
W555	4½" x 4½" jardiniere for 3½" clay pot • 1 dz/shipper/13 lbs	1.75 dz
W556	5½" x 5¼" jardiniere for 4½" clay pot • 1 dz/shipper/18 lbs	2.35 dz
W543/203	5" flower basket/11-hole block • 1 dz/shipper/15 lbs	3.25 dz
W546/205	7" x 3½" flower basket/16-hole block • ½ dz/shipper/13 lbs	4.65 dz

forest green

E3302	3¾" bud • 4 dz/shipper/18 lbs	.75 dz
E3345	6⅜" • 4 dz/shipper/35 lbs	1.10 dz

royal ruby

R3301	4" crimped bud • 4 dz/shipper/17 lbs	.95 dz
E3303	5¾" crimped bud • 4 dz/shipper/20 lbs	.95 dz

18

Vases listed in the 1964 catalog.

Vases listed in the 1964 catalog.

19

Chapter 3
Pitchers and Glasses

Many of the pitchers and glasses included in this chapter have also been listed under the specific pattern. This was done to make this book more "user friendly." I have also included many novelty tumblers, since they are interesting to collect and often provide dates useful in determining when certain patterns were produced. Very few of the Forest Green tumblers have the "anchor over H" emblem embedded in the bottom of the glass.

Left to right: 86 oz. ice lip pitcher #E86, $30-50; 32 oz. giant sized iced tea #E3375, 7", $20-30; 19 oz. large iced tea #E92, 6-1/4", $20-25; 15 oz. straight shell #E3526, 6-5/8", $12-15; 16 oz. iced tea #E69, 6", $12-15, 11 oz. tumbler #E65, 4-3/4", $10-15.

The 1964 catalog listed the #E3526 tumbler.

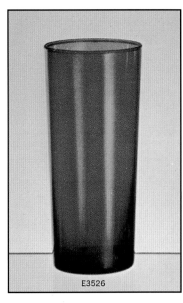

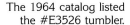
E3526

16 oz. Straight shell #E3526 with applied enamel pussy willows, 6-1/2", $12-15.

16 oz. Straight shell #E3526 with applied enamel marsh grasses, 6-1/2", $12-15.

16 oz. Straight shell #E3526 with applied enamel dogwood flowers, 6-1/2", $12-15.

Square Dance Party Tumbler Set of 16 oz. straight shells #E3526. Left to right: "Do-Si-Do" tumbler, 6-1/2", $10-15; "Hoe Down" tumbler, 6-1/2", $10-15; "Partners all" tumbler, 6-1/2", $10-15; "Swing her high, swing her low" tumbler, 6-1/2", $10-15.

Gay Nineties Set of 16 oz. straight shells #E3526. Left to right: "A Bicycle for Two" tumbler, 6-1/2", $10-15; "Gas Buggy" tumbler, 6-1/2", $10-15; "Open Sleigh" tumbler, 6-1/2", $10-15; "The Harsom" tumbler, 6-1/2", $10-15.

Gay Nineties "Hostess Set" #E1799, $100-125. The box says to "Ship one set with each 1703 Dominion Jumbo Popper-Chef."

The #E1799 "Hostess Set" consists of the four different 16 oz. #E3526 tumblers of the Gay Nineties Series and four Charm 4-5/8" dessert or cereal bowls #E2275.

Dominion Electric Company's Popper-Chef, $50-75.

Closeup of the corn popper lid that was also made by Anchor Hocking as indicated by the Fire-King notation.

Closeup of the label on the Dominion Electric Company's Popper Chef.

16 oz. Straight shell #E3526 with "Surrey with the fringe on top", 6-1/2", $12-15.

Left: 16 oz. Straight shell #E3526 with "Buggy ride", 6-1/2", $12-15; right: 15 oz. straight shell #E3617 with "Buggy ride", 6-1/4", $10-12.

16 oz. Straight shells #E3526 depicting Victorian scenes. Left to right: "East side, west side" tumbler, 6-1/2", $15-20; "On the green" tumbler, 6-1/2", $15-20; "Riding on the mall" tumbler, 6-1/2", $15-20; "Stroll in the park" tumbler, 6-1/2", $15-20.

The Cincinnati Gang

Throughout the years I have come across numerous tumblers with pictures of people surrounded by a variety of signatures. The tumblers were given away in the early 1940s by WLW radio as premium gifts. WLW radio, owned by Crosley Broadcasting Corporation, served the greater Cincinnati, Ohio area. The signatures on the tumblers are placed in different locations on different tumblers. Overall, there are 39 signatures on the fourteen tumblers I found. There may be more, but nobody knows for sure.

The tumblers depict personalities associated with Ruth Lyons, one of the foremost radio hosts of the era. Her show, The 50-50 Club, aired from 12:00 noon to 1:30 p.m. every Monday through Friday. Over the years she received many awards such as the Golden Mike Award, in 1986 she was honored as one of Cincinnati's "Great Living Legends," and was ultimately inducted into the Ohio Women"s Hall of Fame. Ruth passed away in November, 1988, but her memory will live on through the Ruth Lyons Children's Fund. The fund, started in 1939, has raised over 20 million dollars to brighten up the holiday season for hospitalized children.

Many of the signatures on the glasses are very difficult to read, therefore, the spellings below are the best guess for each name. Tumblers have only been located for the names followed by an asterisk.

Rick Hageman*	Henry O'Neill
Howard Chamberlain	Jim P. Shepherd*
Lee Jones	Don Lester
Walter Phillips*	Allan John Esq.
Jim Mood	Jane Lynn*
Joan Whitaker	Dallas DeWeese
Willie Thall*	Charles Resner
Bob Miller	Ruby Wright*
Dave Hamilton	Judy Parkins
Bill Bailey*	Jimmy Crum
Allen Stout	Sally Flowers*
Herb and Kay	Bob Bell
Peter Green*	Bob Provence
Patti O'Hara	Ruth Lyons*
Cliff Lash	Red-Zeke
Betty Ann Horstman*	Pook Buckman*
Paul Crush	Ester Hanlon
Jim Girad	Bonnie Lou*
Dick Bruce*	Waverly Moran
Mariane Spellman	

16 oz. Straight shell Rick Hageman
tumbler, 6-1/2", $12-15.

16 oz. Straight shell Walter Phillips
tumbler, 6-1/2", $12-15.

61

16 oz. Straight shell Willie Thall
tumbler, 6-1/2", $12-15.

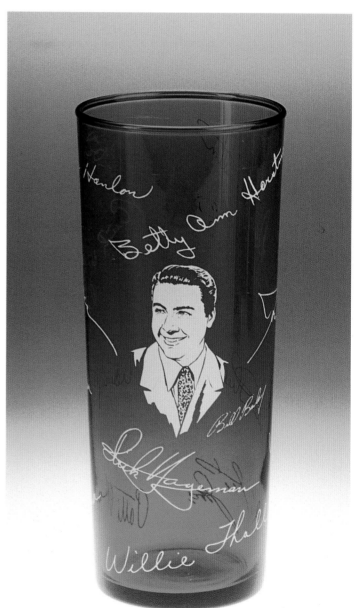

16 oz. Straight shell Bill Bailey
tumbler, 6-1/2", $12-15.

16 oz. Straight shell Peter
Green tumbler, 6-1/2", $12-15.

16 oz. Straight shell Betty Ann
Horstman tumbler, 6-1/2", $12-15.

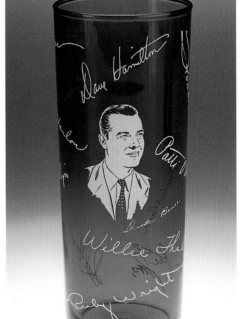

16 oz. Straight shell Dick
Bruce tumbler, 6-1/2",
$12-15.

63

16 oz. Straight shell Jim P. Shepherd tumbler, 6-1/2", $12-15.

16 oz. Straight shell Jane Lynn tumbler, 6-1/2", $12-15.

16 oz. Straight shell Ruby Wright tumbler, 6-1/2", $12-15.

16 oz. Straight shell Sally Flowers tumbler, 6-1/2", $12-15.

16 oz. Straight shell Ruth Lyons tumbler, 6-1/2", $12-15.

16 oz. Straight shell Pook Buckman tumbler, 6-1/2", $12-15.

16 oz. Straight shell Bonnie Lou tumbler, 6-1/2", $12-15.

11 oz. Tumbler #E65 with scenes of Oklahoma, the Sooner State, 4-3/4", $10-12.

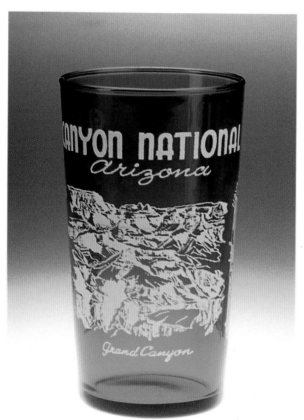

11 oz. Tumbler #E65 with scenes of Grand Canyon National Park, 4-3/4", $10-12.

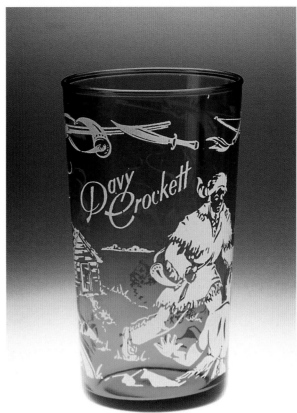

Top left: 11 oz. Tumbler #E65 with scenes of Yellowstone National Park, 4-3/4", $10-12.

Top right: 11 oz. Tumbler #E65 decorated with Davy Crockett, 4-3/4", $20-30.

Forest Green pitchers and tumblers listed in the 1956 catalog.

Forest Green pitchers and tumblers listed in the 1956 catalog.

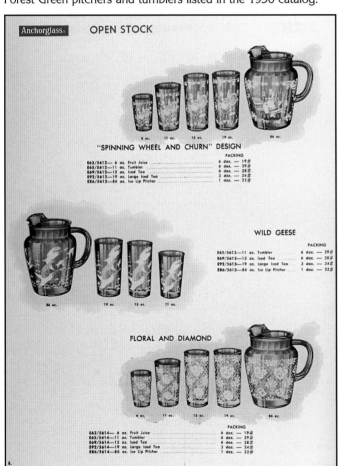

Left to right: 86 oz. Leaf Design ice lip pitcher #E86/351, $50-60; 22 oz. giant
iced tea #E93/351, 6-7/8", $20-30; 11 oz. tumbler #E65/351, 4-3/4", $12-15.

Left to right: 86 oz. Gold and White Vintage ice lip pitcher #E86/5705, $30-50; 32 oz. giant sized iced tea
#E3375/5705, 7", $25-30; 11 oz. tumbler #E65/5705, 4-3/4", $10-15; 6 oz. fruit juice #E 63/5705, 3-3/4", $12-15.

The Gold and White Vintage pattern was also sold as the 7-piece Refreshment Set #E60/282 which consists of one #E86/5705 iced lip pitcher and six 11 oz. tumblers #E65/5705, $100-125 for the complete set.

Left to right: 86 oz. Polka Dot ice lip pitcher #E86/352, $30-50; 32 oz. giant sized iced tea #E3375/352, 7", $20-30; 19 oz. large iced tea #E92/352, 6-1/4", $20-25; 11 oz. tumbler #E65/352, 4-3/4", $10-15.

Unusual Polka Dot 20 oz. tumbler with tapered sides, 6", $20-25.

86 oz. White Lace ice lip pitcher #E86/5807, $50-60.

Another version of the Gazelle 16 oz. straight shell #E3526, 6-5/8", $20-25. Notice this glass has three straight lines at the bottom instead of six wavy lines as on the #E92/5615 tumbler previously shown.

Left: Gazelle 19 oz. large iced tea #E92/5615, 6-1/4", $20-25; right: 11 oz. tumbler #E65/5615, 4-3/4", $10-15.

Comparison of the two version of the Gazelle tumblers. Notice the horns, markings on the body, and position of the gazelle's head are different.

Left: Spinning Wheel and Churn 15 oz. iced tea #E69/5612, 6", $ 15-20; right: 11 oz. tumbler #65/5612, 4-3/4", $10-15. Notice the front and back of the tumblers are different.

Chinese Garden 11 oz. tumbler #E65/590, 4-3/4", $10-15.

Daisey 11 oz. tumbler #E65/496, 4-3/4", $10-15.

White Leaves and Grapes 11 oz. tumbler #E65/370, 4-3/4", $10-15.

Left: Colonial Lady 22 oz. giant iced tea #E93/325, 6-7/8", $20-25; right: 15 oz. iced tea E69/325, 6", $15-20. Notice that the front and back of the tumblers have different colonial scenes.

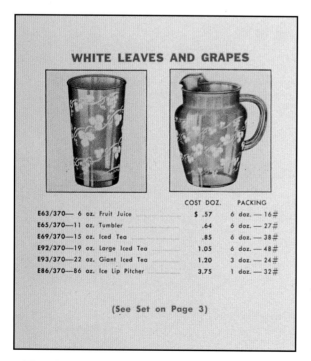

WHITE LEAVES AND GRAPES

	COST DOZ.	PACKING
E63/370— 6 oz. Fruit Juice	$ .57	6 doz. — 16#
E65/370—11 oz. Tumbler	.64	6 doz. — 27#
E69/370—15 oz. Iced Tea	.85	6 doz. — 38#
E92/370—19 oz. Large Iced Tea	1.05	6 doz. — 48#
E93/370—22 oz. Giant Iced Tea	1.20	3 doz. — 24#
E86/370—86 oz. Ice Lip Pitcher	3.75	1 doz. — 32#

(See Set on Page 3)

The 1954 catalog listed the White Leaves and Grapes pitchers and tumblers.

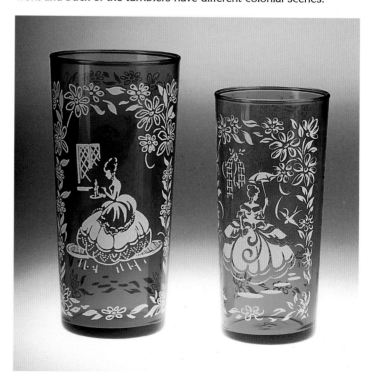

Left: Wild Geese 32 oz. giant sized ice tea #E3375/5613, 7",
$20-30; right: 11 oz. tumbler #E65/5613, 4-3/4", $10-15.

Unusual 20 oz. iced tea #E3369 with applied enamel
snowflakes, 6-7/8", $20-25.

Left: Floral and Diamond 19 oz.
large ice tea #E92/5614, 7", $20-
30; right: 6 oz. fruit juice
#E63/5614, 4-3/4", $10-15.

Plain tapered tumblers. Left to right: 16 oz. tumbler, 5-3/4", $12-15; 12 oz. tumbler #E479, 5-1/4", $10-15; 9 oz. tumbler #E71, 4-1/4", $10-12.

Square Dance Party Tumbler Set consists of 12 oz. tapered tumblers #E479. Left to right: "Do-Si-Do" tumbler, 5-1/4", $10-15; "Hoe Down" tumbler, 5-1/4", $10-15; "Partners all" tumbler, 5-1/4", $10-15; "Swing her high, swing her low" tumbler, 5-1/4", $10-15.

8-Piece set of 12 oz. grape tumblers #E400/76 GRAPE, 5-1/4", $60-75.

8-Piece set of 16 oz. gold leaf tumblers #E400/81 GOLD, 5-3/4", $60-75.

12 oz. Tapered tumblers #E479 with applied enamel cattails and ducks, 5-1/4", $10-12. Notice that the front and back of the tumblers are different.

12 oz. Tapered tumbler #E479 with applied enamel lilies of the valley, 5-1/4", $10-12.

36 oz. Pitcher #E1946, 10", $30-35 and 5 oz. fruit juice #E3653, 3", $5-8. The entire set is etched with tulips, $60-75.

Overhead view showing the arrangement on the pitcher and glasses in the box.

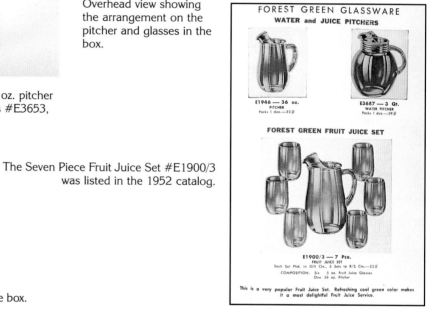

Seven Piece Fruit Juice Set #1900/3 contains one 36 oz. pitcher #E1946, 10", $30-35 and six 5 oz. fruit juice tumblers #E3653, 3", $5-8. The entire set in the original box $75-100.

The Seven Piece Fruit Juice Set #E1900/3 was listed in the 1952 catalog.

Seven Piece Fruit Juice Set #1900/3 removed from the box.

9-1/2 oz. Tall tumbler #E3597, 4-3/4", $10-12. See Whirly Twirly in Chapter 1 for a comparison of this tumbler with the Whirly Twirly pattern.

Left: 9-1/2 oz. tall tumbler #E3321, 4-5/8", $10-12; right: 5 oz. fruit juice #E3323, 3-7/8", $12-15. There is also a 13 oz. iced tea #E3328, 5-1/4" (not shown).

36 oz. Pitcher #E1946 with applied enamel flowers, 10", $40-50.

5 oz. Juice, 3-3/4", $8-10. See Whirly Twirly in Chapter 1 for a comparison of this tumbler with the Whirly Twirly pattern.

Left to right: 15 oz. tumbler, 5-7/8", $10-12; 12 oz. tumbler, 5", $8-10; 5 oz. tumbler, 4 1/8", $8-10.

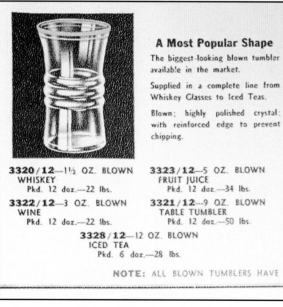

A Most Popular Shape

The biggest-looking blown tumbler available in the market.

Supplied in a complete line from Whiskey Glasses to Iced Teas.

Blown: highly polished crystal: with reinforced edge to prevent chipping.

3320/12—1½ OZ. BLOWN
WHISKEY
Pkd. 12 doz.—22 lbs.

3323/12—5 OZ. BLOWN
FRUIT JUICE
Pkd. 12 doz.—34 lbs.

3322/12—3 OZ. BLOWN
WINE
Pkd. 12 doz.—22 lbs.

3321/12—9 OZ. BLOWN
TABLE TUMBLER
Pkd. 12 doz.—50 lbs.

3328/12—12 OZ. BLOWN
ICED TEA
Pkd. 6 doz.—28 lbs.

NOTE: ALL BLOWN TUMBLERS HAVE

Catalog page listing all five sizes of the flared tumblers in crystal. Not all the sizes were produced in Forest Green or Royal Ruby.

Fairfield 10-1/2 oz. goblet with Forest Green foot (the green coating on the base of the goblet appears yellow when photographed) #E1240, 5-5/8", $20-25.

Rare unopened box containing 36 Fairfield 10-1/2 oz. goblets, $700-750.

The goblets are placed in two layers in the box.

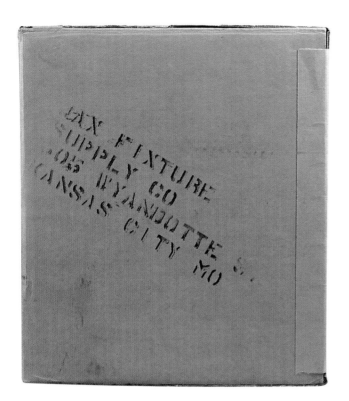

The Fairfield goblets were sold to a fixture supply company in Kansas City, Missouri.

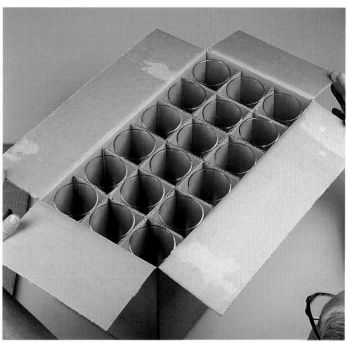

The *1961 Anchor Hocking Institutional Glassware Catalog* listed the #1240 in crystal but it did not list the pattern as Fairfield.

9 oz. Tumbler Set #E71-C, $40-50.

Carrier sets listed in the 1952 catalog.

FOREST GREEN TUMBLERS
TWO VERY POPULAR NUMBERS

SELL AS
OPEN-STOCK
OR IN
SETS OF SIX
AS BELOW

E3597 — 9½ oz.
TALL TUMBLER
Packs 12 doz.—55#

E71 — 9 oz.
TUMBLER
Packs 12 doz.—65#

ALWAYS A GOOD FEATURE
SIX TUMBLERS IN A CARRIER
EASY TO CARRY HOME

E3597-C — 9½ oz.
TUMBLER CARRIER SET
Pkd. 12 Sets to Ctn.—31#
COMPOSITION: Six 9½ oz. Tumblers to a
Set or Carrier

E71-C — 9 oz.
TUMBLER CARRIER SET
Pkd. 12 Sets to Ctn.—38#
COMPOSITION: Six 9 oz. Tumblers to a
Set or Carrier

Tumblers in carriers are a great convenience to you and your customers. Easy to handle in the store and easy to carry home. They naturally suggest a purchase of six or twelve tumblers. Multiple sets like these build sales dollars fast.

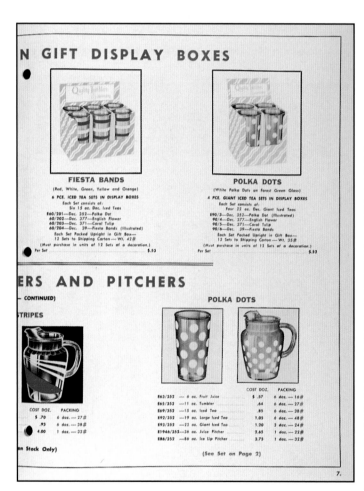

Carrier sets listed in the 1954 catalog.

Carrier sets listed in the 1954 catalog.

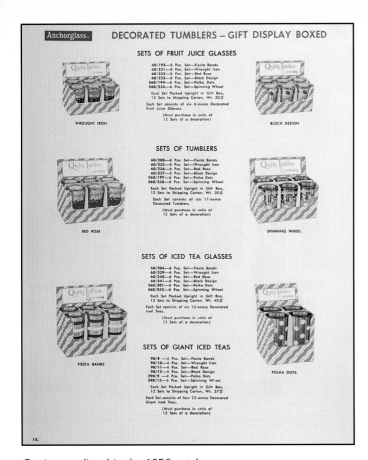

Carrier sets listed in the 1956 catalog.

Carrier sets listed in the 1956 catalog.

10-1/2 oz. Belmont tumbler #E3145, 5", $12-15.

Baltic tumblers. Left: 10 oz. goblet #E3316, 4-1/2", $8-10; right: 5 oz. juice #E3311, 3-5/8", $5-8.

Anchor Hocking listed six pieces of Beverly in the 1971 catalog. I have only been able to find the 4-1/2 oz. cocktail in Royal Ruby and the 9 oz. old fashioned in Forest Green.

Early American. Left to right: 16 oz goblet in crystal, 6", $20-30 in Forest Green; 10 oz. goblet #E336, 5-1/4", $15-20; 4-1/2 oz. fruit juice #E335, 4-1/4", $12-15; 6 oz. sherbet #E333, 4", $12-15; 3-1/2 oz. cocktail #E334, 3-3/8", $18-20.

Georgian 9 oz. tumbler #E49, 4-1/4", $12-15.

Inspiration. Left to right: 13 oz. iced tea, 6-5/8", $15-20; 11 oz. goblet, 5-7/8", $12-15; 4-1/2 oz. juice, 4-1/2", $12-15; 6 oz. sherbet, 3-3/4", $12-15.

Left to right: Milano 3 qt. ice lip pitcher #E4087, $30-40; 12 oz. tumbler #E4012, 5-1/2", $10-12.

Sandwich 36 oz. juice pitcher #E1459, $200-250. There is also a larger 75 oz. ice lip pitcher #E1487, $400-450 (not shown).

Roly Poly. Left to right: 96 oz. upright pitcher #E3687, $40-50; 13 oz. beverage/ice tea #E3658, 5", $8-10; 9 oz. table tumbler #E3651, 4-1/4", $8-10; 5 oz. fruit juice #E3653, 3-3/8", $5-8.

Left: Sandwich 9 oz. tumbler #E1401, 4", $8-10; right: 5 oz. fruit juice #E1403, 3", $5-8.

Windsor 9 oz. tumbler #E1131, 4", $10-12.

Whirly Twirly. Left to right: 3 qt. pitcher #E3587, $50-60; 18 oz. tumbler, 6-1/2", $20-25; 12 oz. tumbler, 5", $15-20; 9 oz. tumbler, 4 1/8", $15-20; 5 oz. tumbler, 3-5/8", $10-12.

Chapter 4
Relish Trays/Lazy Susans

The majority of the relish trays/lazy susans were not sold by Anchor Hocking. They were included in the book because the trays used Old Café inserts. With the exception of the ornate silver set, the crystal, Forest Green, and Royal Ruby inserts are interchangeable in the trays. When the trays were photographed with the Forest Green inserts, they appeared entirely too dark. The decision was made to photograph the trays with the crystal inserts instead. The ornate silver relish set requires the unlined inserts so you can see the engraving in the bottom of the tray. The Forest Green Old Café relish tray inserts must have been made in great quantity.

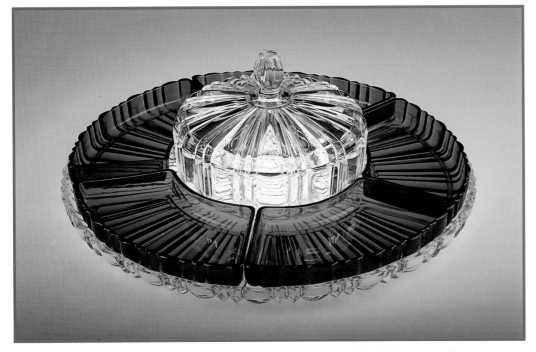

Complete Old Café relish set, $125-150, consists of one 15" crystal plate $30-35, five inserts, $8-10, one #1092 6-3/4" candy jar and cover, $10-15, and one 4" two-piece rotating base, $30-40.

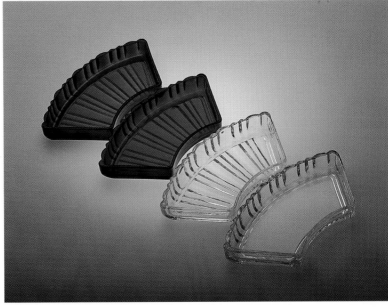

Anchor Hocking made different relish tray inserts: Forest Green, $8-10; Royal Ruby, $8-10; crystal with lines in the bottom, $5-8; crystal with no lines in the bottom, $5-10.

Crystal plate, 15", $30-35. There is a ridge around the clear area in the center of the plate. This ridge holds the base in the tray so the tray doesn't move off center and tip over.

Crystal two-piece rotating base for the relish set, $30-40.

Royal Ruby inserts and crystal covered dish in a stainless steel tray with brass handles (maker unknown). This set does not have a base. The complete set, $75-100. The other colored inserts are interchangeable with the Royal Ruby inserts.

Art deco relish set (maker unknown). The set rotates on a metal base attached to the tray. The railing around the tray is brass. The complete set, $75-100.

Gold and white art deco relish set (maker unknown). This set rotates on a metal base attached to the tray. The complete set, $75-100.

Art deco relish set (maker unknown). The set rotates on a metal base attached to the tray. The railing around the tray is brass. The complete set, $75-100.

Art deco relish set (maker unknown). The set rotates on a metal base attached to the tray. The railing around the tray is brass. The complete set, $75-100.

Ornate silver relish set made by Sheridan Silver Company. The Old Café inserts do not have lines in the bottom so the relish tray engraving is visible. The set rotates on an attached metal base. The complete set, $125-150.

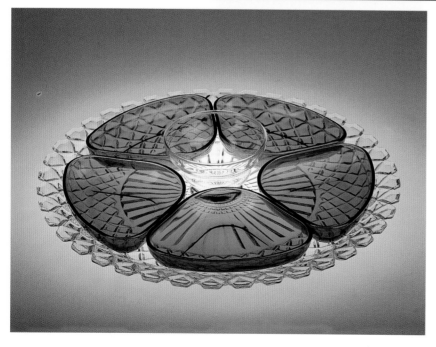

7-Piece Relish Service consisting of one crystal 14" serving plate, five Forest Green relish dishes (inserts), and a crystal sauce cup, $75-100.

7-Piece Relish Service #E2900/100 consisting of one Forest Green 14" serving plate, five Milk White relish dishes (inserts), and a Forest Green sauce cup, $75-100.

Box containing the 7-Piece Relish Service #E2900/100, $25-35 for the box only.

Chapter 5
Lamps

Three different flashed lamps were included in the book. Two of the lamps were hand painted by the Gay Fad Studios of Lancaster, Ohio. Unlike the lamps made with the Royal Ruby vases and ivy balls, I have been unable to locate any true Forest Green lamps.

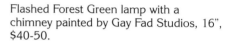

Flashed Forest Green lamp with a shade painted by Gay Fad Studios, 14", $40-50.

Flashed Forest Green lamp with a chimney painted by Gay Fad Studios, 16", $40-50.

Flashed Forest Green lamp with an etched crystal shade, 14", $40-50.

Chapter 6
Bowls

Anchor Hocking made a myriad of bowls as accessory pieces. Most of the items were made in both Forest Green and Royal Ruby. Several of the bowls are extremely plentiful because they were given away with "Junket" Fondant Mix or Quick Fudge Mix.

3-Cornered bon-bons #E159 with and without the "Junket" Fondant Mix labels, 6-1/4", $12-15 without the label; $15-20 with the label.

FREE

With Purchase

1 Pkg.

"JUNKET"
FONDANT MIX

Closeup of the "Junket" Fondant Mix label.

Scalloped bowl #E5069, 6-1/2", $12-15.

Compare the bottom of the crimped bowl #E55 on the left with the scalloped bowl #E5069 on the right.

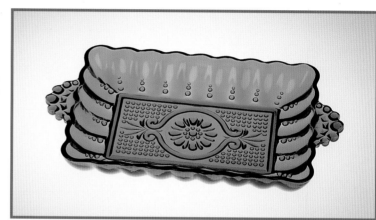

Handled relish tray #E156, 8-1/4" x 4", $20-25.

Crimped bowl #E55, 7-1/2", $15-20.

Crimped bowl #E55 with a manufacturing flaw, 7-1/2", $20-30. Notice the bowl's edge split during the molding process.

Left: Burple bowl #E1878, 8-1/2", $20-30; right: fruit bowl #E1874, 4-5/8", $8-10.

Burple dessert service consisting of one #E1878 bowl and six #E1874 bowls, $60-75.

Left to right: 1-1/2 qt. mixing bowl #E357, 7-1/4", $15-20; 1 qt. mixing bowl #E356, 6", $15-20; 1 pt. Mixing bowl #E 355, 4-7/8", $12-15.

1-1/2 quart mixing bowl #E357 with applied enamel grape leaves, 7-1/4", $20-30.

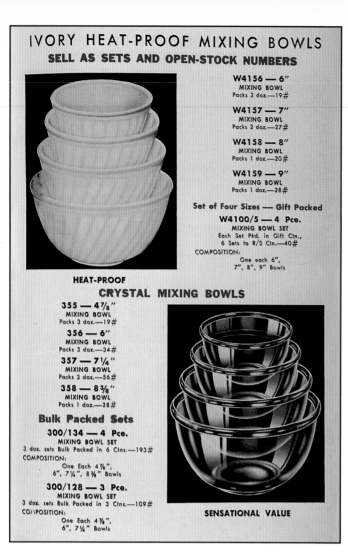

IVORY HEAT-PROOF MIXING BOWLS
SELL AS SETS AND OPEN-STOCK NUMBERS

W4156 — 6"
MIXING BOWL
Packs 2 doz.—19#

W4157 — 7"
MIXING BOWL
Packs 2 doz.—27#

W4158 — 8"
MIXING BOWL
Packs 1 doz.—20#

W4159 — 9"
MIXING BOWL
Packs 1 doz.—28#

Set of Four Sizes — Gift Packed

W4100/5 — 4 Pce.
MIXING BOWL SET
Each Set Pkd. in Gift Ctn.,
6 Sets to R/S Ctn.—40#
COMPOSITION:
One each 6",
7", 8", 9" Bowls

HEAT-PROOF
CRYSTAL MIXING BOWLS

355 — 4⅞"
MIXING BOWL
Packs 3 doz.—19#

356 — 6"
MIXING BOWL
Packs 3 doz.—34#

357 — 7¼"
MIXING BOWL
Packs 3 doz.—56#

358 — 8⅜"
MIXING BOWL
Packs 1 doz.—28#

Bulk Packed Sets

300/134 — 4 Pce.
MIXING BOWL SET
3 doz. sets Bulk Packed in 6 Ctns.—193#
COMPOSITION:
One Each 4⅞",
6", 7¼", 8⅜" Bowls

300/128 — 3 Pce.
MIXING BOWL SET
3 doz. sets Bulk Packed in 3 Ctns.—109#
CO/\POSITION:
One Each 4⅞",
6", 7¼" Bowls

SENSATIONAL VALUE

1969 Catalog listing the four sizes of mixing bowls in crystal.

Splash-Proof bowl #E365, 5-5/8", $15-20.

Bowl #E236, 4-3/4", $20-25.

Tab-handled bowl, 7-5/8", $30-35.

Left: large ribbed bowl, 7", $40-50; right: ribbed bowl #E761, 5", $15-20 with the lid. There is an intermediate sized bowl (not shown) that is 6-1/2" in diameter, $20-25 with the lid. Only the two smaller sizes had crystal lids.

Shell dessert bowl #E11, 7", $10-12.

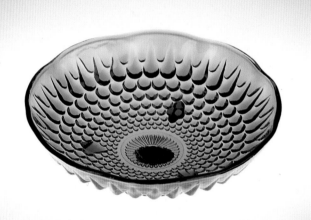

Footed dish #E16, 6-3/8", $15-20.

Leaf and blossom set consists of one 4-1/2" bowl and one #E847 fancy party plate, 8-1/4", $20-30 for the entire set.

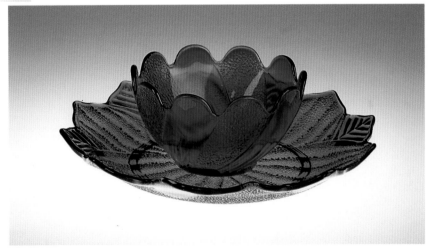

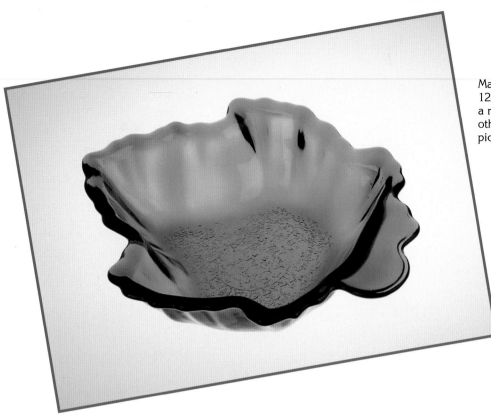

Maple leaf dessert bowl, $10-12. The bottom of the bowl has a rough surface unlike the other version of the bowl pictured.

Maple leaf dessert bowl given away with "Junket" Quick Fudge Mix, $12-15. The bottom surface of the bowl is smooth.

FREE
WITH PURCHASE
OF ONE PACKAGE
"JUNKET"
QUICK FUDGE
MIX

Closeup of the "Junket" Quick Fudge Mix label.

Oval vegetable bowl,
8-1/2" in length, $40-50.

Bowl with horizontal ribs,
$10-20.

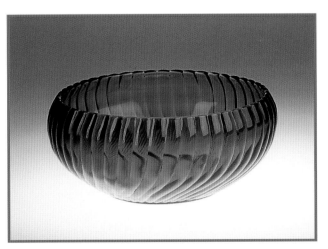

Bulb bowl with vertical ribs,
$10-20.

Chapter 7
Ash Trays

Anchor Hocking catalogs list over 25 types and styles of ash trays. They were made in Crystal, Avocado, Honey Gold, Milk White, Forest Green, and Royal Ruby. I have found the "anchor over H" emblem embedded in the glass on only some of the 5-3/4", 4-5/8", and 3-1/2" square ash trays. The mark is located in one corner of the base.

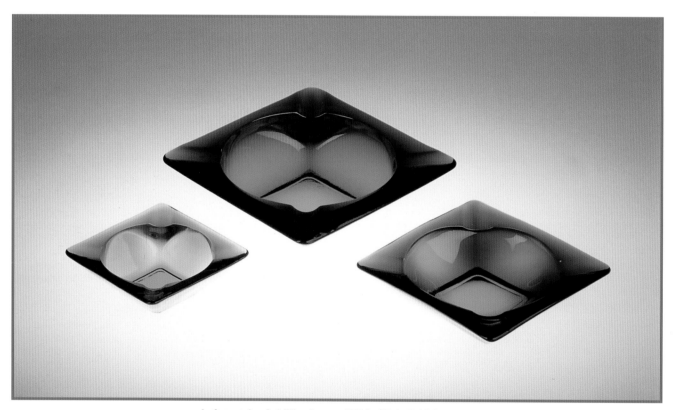

Left to right: 3-1/2" ash tray #E30, $5-8; 5-3/4" ash tray #E32, $10-15; 4-5/8" ash tray #E31, $8-10.

Box containing 3 dozen ash trays #E30, $150-200; $20-25 for the box only.

Box containing 3 dozen ash trays #E31, $200-250; $20-25 for the box only.

Swedish Modern ashtray #E6460, 5" x 5-7/8", $20-30.

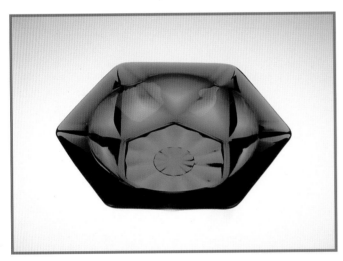

Hexagonal ashtray #E1022, 5-3/4", $15-20.

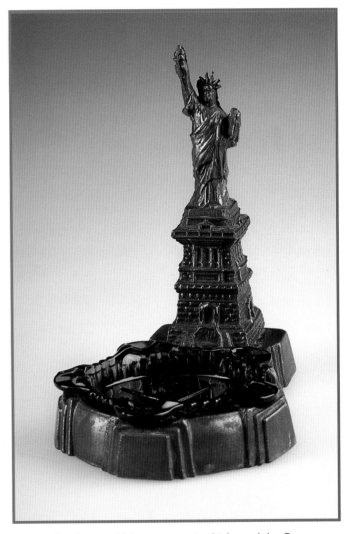

Queen Mary coaster ashtray #E419, 3-1/4", $8-10.

Aftermarket Statue of Liberty souvenir which used the Queen Mary coaster ashtray #E419, $50-75.

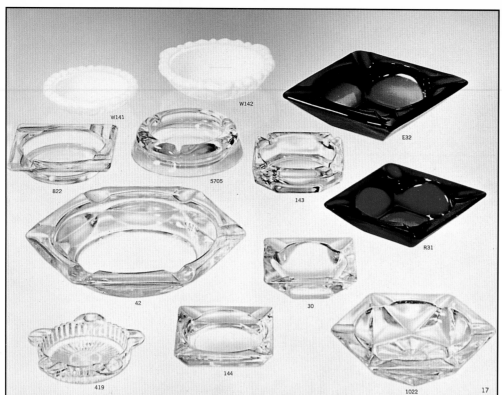

1969 Catalog listing the ashtrays.

W142
W141
822
5705
143
E32
R31
42
30
144
419
1022
17

1969 Catalog listing the ashtrays.

ash trays
sizes, shapes and colors for every need

	30	31	32	143	144	419	822	1022	5705	42	W141	W142
crystal clear	30	31	32	143	144	419	822	1022	5705	42		
royal ruby	R30	R31	R32									
forest green	E30	E31	E32									
milk-white											W141	W142

crystal clear
30	3½" sq • 3 dz/shipper/11 lbs	.60 dz	
31	4⅝" sq • 3 dz/shipper/22 lbs	.90 dz	
32	5¾" sq • 1 dz/shipper/17 lbs	1.75 dz	
143	3⅝" sq deep • 3 dz/shipper/23 lbs	1.20 dz	
144	3½" sq • 6 dz/shipper/21 lbs	.65 dz	
419	3¼" coaster • 6 dz/shipper/19 lbs	.55 dz	

822	4¼" sq • 6 dz/shipper/31 lbs	.75 dz	
1022	5¾" hexagonal • 4 dz/shipper/29 lbs	.85 dz	
5705	4½" smoke ring • 3 dz/shipper/26 lbs	1.50 dz	
42	8½" Diplomat • 1 dz/shipper/21 lbs	3.00 dz	
700/690	4 4" Prescut • gift box • 12 sets/shipper/28 lbs	.50 set	
718-G	7¾" Prescut • gift box • 1 dz/shipper/36 lbs	6.00 dz	

royal ruby
R30	3½" sq • 3 dz/shipper/11 lbs	.95 dz
R31	4⅝" sq • 3 dz/shipper/23 lbs	1.65 dz
R32	5¾" sq • 1 dz/shipper/17 lbs	2.40 dz

forest green
E30	3½" sq • 3 dz/shipper/11 lbs	.60 dz
E31	4⅝" sq • 3 dz/shipper/23 lbs	.90 dz
E32	5¾" sq • 1 dz/shipper/17 lbs	1.75 dz

milk-white
W141	4¼" round • 4 dz/shipper/17 lbs	.75 dz
W142	5¼" round • 2 dz/shipper/14 lbs	1.15 dz

700/690
718-G

16

Diplomat ashtray #E42, 8-1/2", $40-50. This ashtray has a winter scene attached to the back and the entire back of the ashtray is covered with gold foil.

100

Chapter 8
Miscellaneous/Novelty Items

Throughout the period of 1940 to 1964, Anchor Hocking made countless novelties in Forest Green. Very few were trademarked in the glass. The majority of the pieces were marked with paper labels. Also included in this chapter are items that didn't seem to fit in any other chapter.

Catalog page listing the apothecary jars made by Anchor Hocking.

Flashed Forest Green 22 oz. stemmed candy jar/cover #E3291, 10", $50-60.

The apothecary jars were shipped in plastic tubes. This is the only shipping tube I have ever seen and it was used to ship a frosted apothecary jar.

1955 Anchor Hocking sales brochure listing the Serva-Snack sets with Forest Green cups.

Serva-Snack tray, $4-5; 5 oz. cup, $2-4.

Serva-Snack tray, $4-5; 5 oz. cup, $2-4.

Serva-Snack tray, $4-5; 5 oz. cup, $2-4.

Eight-Piece Serva-Snack Set #E200/36 with four Forest Green cups and four fan-shaped crystal trays, $40-50.

Overhead view of the set so you can see the arrangement of the cups and plates.

14-Piece Punch Set consists of one 10" punch bowl, one punch bowl base, and twelve punch cups #E279 (only six shown), $100-125 for the complete set.

Punch bowl base, $30-35.

Punch cup #E279, $2-4.

The popcorn bowl has a diameter of 5-1/4" and the glass is very thick, $12-15.

The popcorn set consists of one 10" popcorn bowl (punch bowl without the base), $35-50, and eight 5-1/4" bowls, $12-15; $90-100 for the complete set.

Extremely rare Forest Green throw-away beer bottle, mold #8565A, 6-3/4", $200-250.

Ribbed water bottle with lid, 8", $65-75.

Large storage jar with aluminum cover probably made by Anchor Hocking, 7-1/2" in diameter and 7-3/4" in height, $35-50. This storage container can also be found with a glass lid or fitted with a vaporizer.

One gallon jar #E274, 8", $65-75.

Forest Green flashed piggy bank #E5068, 5" in height, 6" in length, $20-30.

Fish bowl probably made by Anchor Hocking, 5-1/4" x 9-1/2", $30-40.

Paperweight, 2" x 3-1/2", $150-200.

Paperweight, 3-3/8" x 4-3/8", $75-100. The bottom of the paperweight states "Salem NJ est. 1675 by John Fenwick, 1642 – 1694."

One gallon Rex Ray Vaporizer distributed by the Rexall Drug Company, $40-50.

Closeup of the label on the Rex Ray Vaporizer.

Chapter 9
Confusing Similarities

Over the last couple of years I have noticed some confusion as to what constitutes Royal Ruby or Forest Green. Two types of glass are often confused with Anchor Hocking's glassware. The first is Wheaton Glass Company's Bullseye pattern. This glass, produced in the early 1970s, mimics most of the colors of Anchor Hocking glass. This pattern is available in five colors and was produced as glasses, mugs, creamers and sugars, cruets, vases, salt and pepper shakers, and candlesticks. The second, Arcoroc glass from France, is also often mistaken as Royal Ruby or Forest Green. This glassware can still be purchased at Wal-Mart, K-Mart, and other similar stores. The glassware is available in plates, cups and saucers, bowls, and several sizes of glasses. All of the pieces are marked with "Made in France."

Left to right: Bullseye vases in red, green, and yellow, 9", $10-15 each.

Left: Bullseye sugar, 4", $20-30; right: creamer, 4", $12-15.

Left : Bullseye glass, 5", $10-12; right: Bullseye glass, 4", $10-12.

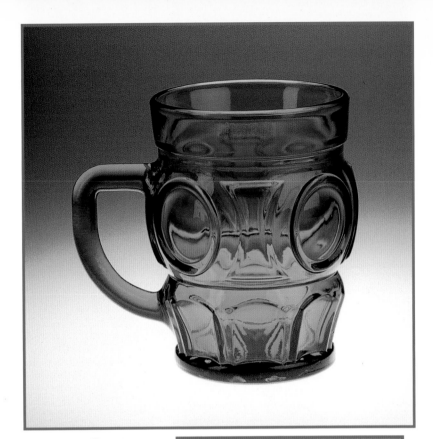

Bullseye coffee mug,
4", $10-12.

Bullseye cruet, 8" to
the top of the stopper,
$20-30 each.

Grecian style vase
made by Wheaton
Glass Company, 9",
$8-10.

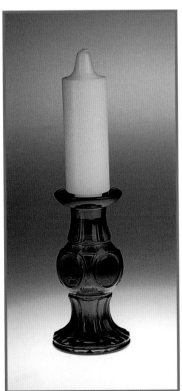

Bullseye candleholder,
4-3/4", $12-15 each.

Green glass made by Arcoroc in France. This glassware is available in a variety of glasses, plates, and other dinnerware.

NAPCO made a myriad of items in green glass. There are at least two sizes of these items that are either napkin holders or storage containers.

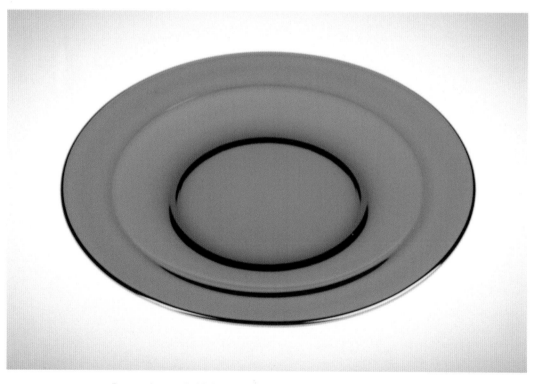

Green plate with 22 kt. gold trim of unknown origin, 8-1/2".

Chapter 10
Advertising Sheets

Information about the production of Anchor Hocking glassware is limited. I was able to obtain certain "jobber" sheets that were distributed in place of catalogs. Anchor Hocking relied on these sheets from 1945 to the middle 1950s. After that, catalogs were published and distributed. Some rare advertising proofs are also included. If you look carefully on the bottom of the proofs, you will see a list of the magazines or trade publications where the ad would appear. Many of these trade publications are obscure and haven't been published for years.

Advertising proof sheet created by Anchor Hocking's Advertising Department. It is a rare piece of Anchor Hocking documentation. Notice the list of trade publications where the advertisement would appear.

Advertising proof sheet created by Anchor Hocking's Advertising Department. It is a rare piece of Anchor Hocking documentation. Notice the list of publications where the advertisement would appear.

The actual advertisement as it appeared in *Good Housekeeping*. Forest Green items listed in the 1952 catalog.

Advertisement found in the September 1955 *Life Magazine*

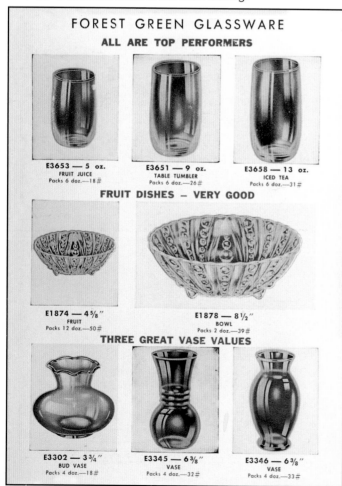

FOREST GREEN GLASSWARE
ALL ARE TOP PERFORMERS

E3653 — 5 oz.
FRUIT JUICE
Packs 6 doz.—18#

E3651 — 9 oz.
TABLE TUMBLER
Packs 6 doz.—26#

E3658 — 13 oz.
ICED TEA
Packs 6 doz.—31#

FRUIT DISHES – VERY GOOD

E1874 — 4⅝"
FRUIT
Packs 12 doz.—50#

E1878 — 8½"
BOWL
Packs 2 doz.—39#

THREE GREAT VASE VALUES

E3302 — 3¾"
BUD VASE
Packs 4 doz.—18#

E3345 — 6⅜"
VASE
Packs 4 doz.—32#

E3346 — 6⅜"
VASE
Packs 4 doz.—33#

Index

Apothecary Jars, 101
Ash Trays, 27, 38, 98-100
Baltic, 11-12
Beer Bottles, 104
Belmont, 13
Beverly, 14
Bowls, 91-97
Bubble, *See Provincial*
Bullseye, 108-109
Burple, 15
Charm, 16-17
Corn Popper, 58
Early American, 18-19
Factory Sheets, 111-112
Georgian, 20
Glasses, 55-84
Inspiration, 21-22
Lamps, 90
Lazy Susans, 85-86

Lido, 23
Milano, 23
Novelty Items, 101-107
Pitchers, 55-84
Provincial, 24-26
Punch set, 103-104
Queen Mary, 27
Relish Sets, 85-89
Roly Poly, 28-32
Sandwich, 33-36
Serva-Snack Sets, 102
Swedish Modern, 37-38
Tumblers, *see Glasses*
Vases, 45-54
Water Bottles, 105
Waterford, 39-40
Whirly Twirly, 41-43
Windsor, 44